THE PRECIOUS PEARL
A Translation from the Arabic

HARVARD UNIVERSITY
CENTER FOR THE STUDY OF WORLD RELIGIONS

Studies in World Religions

edited by
Jane I. Smith

Studies in World Religions publishes monographs, translations, and collections of essays by persons who have been or are affiliated with Harvard's Center for the Study of World Religions, as well as proceedings of Center-sponsored conferences and colloquia.

Number 1

THE PRECIOUS PEARL
A Translation from the Arabic
by
Jane Idleman Smith

THE PRECIOUS PEARL
A Translation from the Arabic

Jane Idleman Smith

Scholars Press

Distributed by
Scholars Press
PO Box 5207
Missoula, Montana 59806

THE PRECIOUS PEARL
A Translation from the Arabic with Notes
of the
Kitāb al-Durra al-Fākhira fī Kashf ʿUlūm al-Ākhira
of Abū Ḥāmid Muḥammad b. Muḥammad b. Muḥammad
al-Ghazālī

Jane Idleman Smith

Library of Congress Cataloging in Publication Data

al-Ghazzali, 1058-1111.
The precious pearl.

(Monograph series - Center for the Study of World Religions, Harvard University ; no. 1)
Translation of al-Durrah al-ṭākhirah fī kashf 'ulūm al-Ākhirah.
Bibliography: p.
Includes index.
1. Future life (Islam) 2. Judgement Day (Islam) I. Title. II. Series: Harvard University. Center for the Study of World Religions. Monograph series - Center for the Study of World Religions, Harvard University ; no. 1.
BP166.8.G4713 1979 297'.23 79-140
ISBN 0-89130-278-6
ISBN 0-89130-305-7 pbk.

Printed in the United States of America

1 2 3 4 5

Edwards Brothers, Inc.
Ann Arbor, MI 48104

TABLE OF CONTENTS

PREFACE

One of the valuable products of the mid-twentieth century's increased concern for the comparative history of world religions is the correspondingly increased availability of many documents and works hitherto accessible only to scholars of particular traditions. At the same time that comparative studies are proliferating on a variety of topics, the large number of translations of sacred and secondary texts allows students of the history of religion to enhance their understanding by the examination of primary source materials. It is hoped that the following translation of a text thus far unavailable to Western students in English will help to supplement the growing pool of translations of Islamic works.

The text used was that from which Lucien Gautier made his French translation La Perle Precieuse de Ghazālī (see Introduction below). Any material added to the text in the way of brief explanation, verse references to the Qur'ān, addition of an Arabic word in question or its alternative translations, has been given in square brackets. Round brackets are used for that material actually in the text but which seems to be a kind of aside or footnote or interruption of the narrative of the author himself. Verses or parts of verses from the Qur'ān (given in the Arabic, of course, without punctuation) are set off in the translation by round brackets and stars, ✱...✱, with the reference in square brackets following to the location of the material in the Azhar 1337 edition of the Qur'ān (S signifying Sura). Unless otherwise stated, all page references in the supplementary materials are to the pages of the text itself rather than to the page numbers of this translation; the page numbers of the text are inserted into the body of the translation between parallel lines.

I would like to express my gratitude to the members of the Editorial Board of "Studies in World Religions", and to Ellen Lieberson and William Darrow of the staff of the Center for the Study of World Religions, for their contribution to the preparation of this work for publication. I am especially grateful to John Alden Williams for reading the text and offering valuable suggestions. Needless to say, I am responsible for the form in which the translation now stands, as well as for any errors that it might contain.

Jane I. Smith
Harvard University

INTRODUCTION

There are no major religions of the world that do not have a concern for questions of life after death, although many do not treat it in as detailed a way as have the theologians and traditionists of Islam. The Qur'ān, of course, leads the way with a startling revelation of a cataclysmic eschaton and judgment of individual souls radically opposed to the vague and often contradictory beliefs of pre-Islamic Arabia. Thus we read in *sūra* 16:38, "They [those of the pagan Arabs who scoffed at the message of the Prophet] swear to the limit of their oaths that God will not raise up again those who die....". But the assurance of the Qur'ān is that "When the sun is folded up, and the stars fall down, and when the mountains are set in motion...when the seas are fired up to a boil...when the scrolls are laid open, when the sky is torn away, when the Fire is kindled and the Garden is brought nigh, then shall a soul know what it has prepared [for itself]." [S 81:1-14]

The Qur'ānic descriptions of these events have been greatly elaborated by the traditions, and many details have been supplied there that are lacking in the account of the Book. Some of these are supported by strong and reliable chains of transmission, while many are considered by scholars of Islam to be weak and of dubious authenticity. Such lack of scholarly sanction, however, has done little to discourage their acceptance into the general fabric of beliefs of many generations of faithful Muslims. Even today one finds that rationalism, skepticism, and the rejection of *taqlīd* [uncritical acceptance of tradition] do not deter many a pious Muslim from affirming the realities of the chastisement of the grave and the physical pleasures of the Garden.

As a self-consciously historical religion, Islam bases its well-developed conceptions of the afterlife upon a clear framework of the understanding of time and its progression. In this context the descriptions of events occurring in relation to individuals and communities after death fall into two categories: (1) those coming between individual death and final resurrection and (2) the series of events that signals the end of historical time, namely the arrival of the eschaton or the Hour, the specifics of individual judgment and consignment to felicity or perdition that marks the transition from time to eternity. For the most part the detailed particulars of both periods are non-Qur'ānic and their articulation has undergone a series of additions, revisions, and modifications. It is in the first category, however, that one might look for the most obvious incursions of local beliefs and attitudes into the general fabric of Islamic theology. The Qur'ān itself is so articulate and impressive in its characterization of the occurrences of the second period that the traditions have been able to add only detail, not drama, to it. Some details elaborate, some are specifically new.

The Qur'ān has long been available to Western readers in translation. Anyone who has read the original Arabic, however, can understand and appreciate the general Muslim feeling that on the theological plane as God's word and revelation it is ultimately untranslatable, and that on the linguistic level the richness and versatility of the Arabic make an adequate rendering into another language extremely difficult. Nonetheless, the general outline of the Qur'ānic instruction concerning eschatology has been understood by non-Arabic students of Islam. This has been much less true of the materials concerning the period immediately after death and the elaboration of details on the eschaton. Traditions have been cited randomly and full texts on the theme of the afterlife have been difficult of access.

Several happy exceptions to this, however, have been extant for about a century. One is the German translation by M. Wolff of an anonymous work entitled *Kitāb aḥwāl al-qiyāma* (published in Leipzig in 1892 as *Muhammedanische Eschatologie*). The material in this text deals primarily with popular traditions concerning resurrection, judgment, and descriptions of the Garden and the Fire. (This work is identical in almost every detail with Imam ʿAbd al- Raḥīm ibn Aḥmad al-Qāḍī's *Daqā'iq al-akhbār fī dhikr al-janna wa'l-nār*, translated into English by ʿĀ'isha ʿAbd al-Raḥmān and published under the title *The Islamic Book of the Dead*, 1977.)

The other major work available in a Western translation is the French rendering by Lucien Gautier of the present text attributed to Abū Ḥāmid al-Ghazālī, published originally in 1878 as *La Perle Precieuse de Ghazālī*. (A German translation of this same text was made by M. Brugsch, entitled *Die kostbare Perle über Tod und Jenseits*.) Recently large portions of John Macdonald's translation of Abū'l-Layth al-Samarqandī's eleventh century *hijrī* manuscript on death and resurrection, *Kitāb ḥaqā'iq al-daqā'iq* with accompanying interpretations have been made available in the journal *Islamic Studies* (1964-65). This last is a particularly welcome addition to Western scholarship, as it provides English speaking students with a readable translation put into the context of a well-documented analysis of the factors contributing to the development of this kind of eschatological literature.

It is the intention of the present translation of the *Durra al-fākhira* not necessarily to improve on that done by Gautier, but rather to make available to those for whom English is the primary language a text extremely important for an understanding of Islamic eschatology. Many students of religion in general, who are not necessarily specialists in the study of Islam, are coming to be interested in the comparative study of original texts.

It seems particularly important not only to provide them with materials that illustrate individual points of theology and tradition, but to supplement those materials with some basic information about the religion of Islam in general. The notes to the following translation attempt to make the text comprehensible to the general reader as well, hopefully, as instructive to the specialist. As more texts from other traditions are translated and analyzed, the student of comparative conceptions of the afterlife will have an increasingly rich store of primary materials available in English.

Perhaps no figure in the history of Islamic theology and philosophy has so captured the imagination of non-Muslims as has Abū Ḥāmid Muḥammad b. Muḥammad b. Muḥammad al-Ghazālī of Ṭūs (450/1058-505/1111). Revered by Muslims throughout the ages, al-Ghazālī also has been disclaimed by such groups as certain of the philosophers and the Bāṭinīya. He demonstrated in his life and thought a breadth of knowledge and concern which in itself perhaps led to some of the criticism leveled against him by his co-religionists. To the philosophers he was a theologian, to the theologians he often showed himself too deeply concerned with philosophy; and though he found the goal of his agonizing quest for truth in the fold of Islamic mysticism, he has seldom been classed with the greatest or most profound of the Sufis. Nevertheless he is generally recognized by Muslims and non-Muslims alike as the great reconciler of divergent trends in Islam, whose skill in rational analysis and theological disputation combined with his intense personal piety have seldom been equalled in any one person.

Largely because of al-Ghazālī's own characterization in his autobiography *Munqidh min al-ḍalāl*, it has been popular to view his life as a series of encounters with dominant trends in Islamic thinking. This is traditionally seen as ending with the great realization that it is only through *dhawq*, the "taste" of the mystical experience, that final satisfaction is attained. The actual progression of events in his life, however, was not nearly so clear-cut. He lived at a time when Ismā^cīlī Shī^cism was a political as well as ideological threat to Sunnī orthodoxy and when the encounters between *falsafa* and *kalām* (which can only somewhat loosely be translated as philosophy and scholastic theology) were sharp and somewhat virulent. His earliest education was at the hands of a Sufi friend of his father, and the lessons there learned seem never to have left him. The crowning work of a prolific, as well as personally agonizing, career is the magnificant Iḥyā' [c]ulūm al-dīn, or Revivification of the Sciences of Religion.

It is interesting to note that many of the details recited in the Durra al-fākhira seem to be a repetition or reworking of material presented first in the last book of the Iḥyā', as the author himself indicates frequently in the text. This tells us, of course, that the Durra was written after the Iḥyā', if indeed by al-Ghazālī, toward the end of the author's career and life. Western scholars have been far from unanimous in attributing authenticity to this work as actually coming from the pen of al-Ghazālī. M. Asin Palacios (La Espiritualidad de Algazal) and W. Montgomery Watt ("The authenticity of the words attributed to al-Ghazālī", JRAS 1952), for example, feel that apparent inconsistency with some of al-Ghazālī's other works is sufficient to warrant skepticism; Hava Lazarus-Yafeh is even stronger in her opinion that the Durra must not be considered to be among the works of al-Ghazālī (Studies in al-Ghazzali). Others such as Margaret Smith (Al-Ghazālī the Mystic), Ignaz Goldziher (Die Richtungen der islamischen Koranauslegung) and Lucien Gautier opt for its authenticity, as do most contemporary Muslim scholars. The present introduction is presented on the assumption that, recent Orientalist scholarship notwithstanding, the Durra reasonably may be seen as consonant with, if not an exact record of, al-Ghazālī's thoughts on questions of ethical responsibility and the afterlife. Whether or not it came from the same source as the Iḥyā', it stands as a classical example of a medieval manual on matters of life after death, and one that centuries of Muslims have attributed to Abū Ḥāmid.

The narrative of the Durra is an interesting combination of flow and digression, as if the author were trying to communicate a basic theme but were actually more concerned with the supporting materials than with the main message of the text. For the most part, little background is needed to grasp what is being expressed. A word, however, ought to be said about the understanding of the structure of the universe and levels of reality.

The Qur'ān speaks several times of the basic sevenfold structure of the heavens: ❛He it is Who created the seven heavens...❜ [S 67:3]; ❛We have built over you the seven firmaments [*sabᶜan shidādan*]...❜ [S 78:12]. The author of this text (whom for purposes of convenience we will here assume to be al-Ghazālī) recognizes this structure, and explicitly makes reference to it in his descriptions of the journey of the soul immediately after death through the seven heavens, based on the *miᶜrāj* or heavenly night journey of the Prophet. Later he describes the angels of the seven heavens surrounding the dead in concentric circles at the time of resurrection. More important to the development of his text than this, however, is the idea of the three worlds or planes of existence. In the beginning of the Durra he makes reference to the earthly world [*al-ᶜālam al-dunyawī*] and to the *malakūtī* and *jabarūtī* (see note 4 of the text below) worlds. The first refers to Adam and his descendants and the three classes of animals. The second is comprised of the angels and *jinn* and the third of the elect among the angels.

Now the fact of a tripartite division of reality as well as of spiritual states is common to much of al-Ghazālī's writing. But it is interesting to note the order in which he places them in the Durra (which might well be adduced as another argument for its non-authenticity as a work of al-Ghazālī). In the Iḥyā' the general understanding is that the earthly world is the world of sense perception, the second or intermediate or celestial world (the world of the traveller on the way who has made some progress but not yet reached his destination) is called *ᶜālam al-jabarūt*, and the divine world, the highest of the three, is the *ᶜālam al-malakūt*. In the Durra, however, the more common Islamic ranking of these spheres is followed, placing the *jabarūtī* realm as the highest. Thus it is in the *malakūtī* world that are found those modalities of judgment that are too gross for the highest and most spiritual world, but whose reality al-Ghazālī does not want actually to deny, such as the balance and the existence of the Qur'ān and Islam and Friday as personalities. (This is not unambiguous, however, for we also find the Qur'ān has a *jabarūtī* existence as a personality.) The designations, of course, are in themselves not significant, and in fact they are occasionally interchanged by other writers such as the Neo-Platonic philosophers al-Fārābī and Ibn Sīna, by whom al-Ghazālī was influenced. The point of note is the way in which cosmology is coordinated with the spiritual journey for al-Ghazālī, and how he uses the intermediate level as a means of giving credence to aspects of the judgment which are difficult to reconcile with a more deeply mystical understanding.

The author of this text clearly accepts the basic articles of faith concerning the life after death to which Islamic orthodoxy gives credence. The writing in general does not reflect much in the way of esoteric interpretation; in the tripartite structure, however, one finds room for the mystical understanding that passes beyond the particulars dominating the traditional Muslim treatment of eschatology. As he expressly states in the text (pp. 69-70) he does not actually favor an allegorical interpretation of the *ḥadīth*s relating to the judgment, and certainly never denies the reality of the Garden or the Fire. If one put this work in the context of others of al-Ghazālī's writings, particularly the Iḥyā', it would appear that he holds in balance the *ẓāhir* and the *bāṭin*, the exoteric and the esoteric understandings of reality. For al-Ghazālī the Fire and the Garden are finally to be understood as mystical states of separation from or union with God, although this is far from explicit in this particular work.

The Durra, in fact, actually stops short of any real consideration of the nature of heaven and hell, more accurately expressed in their exact translation as the Garden and the Fire. Both are present in their personified forms at the awesome time of the judgment, but conspicuously absent are the descriptions of the pavilions of paradise and the sensual pleasures of the *ḥūr* so evident in most eschatological writings, as well as many specifics of the torments of damnation. The author himself offers no obvious explanation of this; it is as if the reader were led through the progression of personal history (the immediate experiences in the tomb after death) and the communal history (in the final events of the arrival of the Hour and the judgment), but cut off from narrative at the precise point where history becomes eternity -- where, in fact, no more moral and ethical lessons can be drawn.

Here, it seems, may lie the real explanation of the author's approach to the material and his continual interruption of the text to offer specific cases and examples. Gautier in his introduction says, "Dans la Dourra, il a voulu probablement reproduire sous une forme plus brève et plus populaire ses enseignements relatifs à la vie future." (p. xvi) It seems equally apparent, however, that the author was presenting a series of ethical teachings that are intended less as descriptions of the future life than as injunctions for the living of this life in order to be ready for the events of the Day and the Hour. This is not to say that he fails to elaborate in extremely graphic terms events that will come to pass. His description of God's appearance on the day of resurrection, twirling the heavens and the earths on His fingertips crying, "I am the King ...to whom belongs the kingdom today if not to me!" is tremendously exciting narrative. But behind it all one senses the equally powerful urgency to impress upon his readers the need to stop and make a decision *now* as to how to live life, as al-Ghazālī himself was so dramatically forced to do when God took from him his own power of speech and he had to retire from his teaching. The text is almost deceptively straightforward, but the clues to this kind of urgency can be found in such simple asides as his injunction (p. 28) to "Do the work to which God has guided you, that there may be a special camel [the beast created out of one's good works that carry him to the resurrection] for you alone, and know that such is a profitable enterprise!"

* * *

There are a number of versions of this text entitled *al-Durra al-fākhira fī ᶜulūm al-ākhira* (see Brockelmann, *GAS*, S 1 746). To Lucien Gautier, in his French translation *La Perle Precieuse*, goes the credit for having worked through eight separate manuscripts (see pp. xi-xvi of his introduction for a description of these texts and their variations). His own translation was based on a collation of these several manuscripts; the text so established is printed with the French translation, with extensive footnotes indicating possible alternative readings. Western scholarship over the last century has taken his compilation and translation to be as lucid and as accurate a rendering of the author's original work as we reasonably can hope to attain. This present translation into English, then, is of the text he offers as representing a majority opinion of the several manuscripts with which he worked, taking into consideration as well the possible variations he presented. Considering the work as a whole, the alternative readings seldom seem to make a significant difference in the basic understanding of the text. The student of Arabic wishing to trace for himself the possible variants is invited to refer to Gautier's now classic rendition.

This work is much less theoretical than is al-Ghazālī in others of his writings, and makes much use of stories and traditions. Many of these traditions are common to the lore of Islam, particularly those giving details of the period immediately after death and the events of the eschaton. The only collection of *ḥadīth*s to which he makes specific reference is al-Jāmiᶜ al-ṣaḥīḥ of Abū ᶜAbd Allāh Muḥammad b. Ismāᶜīl al-Bukhārī, one of the six major compilations of traditional material. The reader wishing to consult other collections or to check particular points in the Arabic literature is referred to A. J. Wensinck's Concordance et indices de la tradition musulmane. Occasional footnotes to this translation suggest correlative traditions; the works from which these samples are taken are listed in the bibliography at the end of the translation, with abbreviations in brackets.

Two other aids are provided here to help the reader to find particular material in the text quickly. One is the index at the end, consisting principally of proper names and Arabic terms. The other is a kind of topical index preceding the text in the form of an outline (not, of course, part of the original Arabic). The author divides his work into nine parts or chapters [*fuṣūl*], for which the text outlines gives appropriate manuscript pages and a content breakdown. The last chapter or *faṣl* begins only slightly past the middle of the text, and apparently continues until the end. Because of the length of this section, smaller unit breakdowns are given with appropriate page numbers in the outline. It is hoped that with this kind of outline the reader may be able to have an overview of the flow of this work that is somewhat difficult to get from reading the text itself, due to the author's tendency to interrupt his own narrative.

Death for al-Ghazālī, as he repeats in many ways in the Iḥyā', means essentially the separation of the soul from the body, the abandoning by the soul of the cares and confinements of this world. It is obvious here that for those who know, whose light is strong (see p. 46 and note 80), death is to be desired. And yet, as the author explains so graphically in this text, such is the complex make-up of every individual that all share in the dread of death, and none is free from the accompanying terrors of the final judgment. The theme to which al-Ghazālī continually returns, however, is that of the freeing of the soul from the body, the comparison of death with the sleep of this world from which the awakening will be, for the pious and knowledgeable, eternal abiding in the presence of God.

As is to be expected, one does not find in the text an explicit statement of the meaning of "the precious pearl". Anyone familiar with the thought of al-Ghazālī, however, can see in it an abvious reference to the human soul. It seems appropriate to set the scene for the treatment of the adventures of that soul as described in the Durra by quoting from verses attributed to al-Ghazālī in another context. These are given in full translation by Margaret Smith in her classic work Al-Ghazālī the Mystic (pp. 36-37, from Brit. Mus. Add. 76561) with the note that these were, according to tradition, the last words to have been put on paper by al-Ghazālī before he gave himself up to death (Smith notes that while they are sometimes actually attributed to Aḥmad al-Ghazālī, they are also to be found in Abū Ḥāmid's _Taḥsīn al-ẓunūn_):

"Say to my friends, when they look upon me, dead,
Weeping for me and mourning for me in sorrow
Do not believe that this corpse you see is myself.
In the name of God, I tell you, it is not I,
I am a spirit, and this is naught but flesh.
It was my abode and my garment for a time.
I am a treasure, by a talisman kept hid,
Fashioned of dust, which served me as a shrine,
I am a pearl, which has left its shell deserted,
It was my prison, where I spent my time in grief.

Think not that death is death, nay, it is life,
A life that surpasses all we could dream of here,
While in this world. Here we are granted sleep,
Death is but sleep, sleep that shall be prolonged.
Be not affrighted when death draweth nigh,
It is but the departure for this blessed home.
Think of the mercy and love of your Lord,
Give thanks for His grace and come without fear.
What I am now, even so shall you be,
For I know that you are even as I am.
The souls of all men came forth from God,
The bodies of all are compounded alike
Good and evil, alike it was ours.
I give you now a message of good cheer
May God's peace and joy for evermore be yours."

TEXT OUTLINE

Pages of the Text:

1-3 Introduction and classification of worlds and creatures.

3-4 Chapter [One]. God's initial division of men into those destined for the Garden and those destined for the Fire; the primordial covenant; the breath of life in the womb.

4-17 Chapter [Two]. The departure of the soul at death; the good and the wicked; the agony of death; temptations presented to the dying; the guidance of Gabriel; the way in which the dying lose their faculties; the ascent of the good soul through the seven heavens in the company of Gabriel; some of the dead seen in dreams relating their experiences before God in this ascent.

17-27 Chapter [Three]. The experiences of the profligate at death; the brief ascent of the profligate soul and expulsion to Sijjīn; the fate of Christians and Jews; different categories of negligent believers; return of the soul to the place where the body is being washed; interment of the body and the visit of the angel Rūmān; the two interrogating angels; personification of the deeds of the individual souls.

27-32 Chapter [Four]. Interrogation of the souls of the profligate and personification of their deeds; vision of dead in dreams and instructions given by the dead to the living; visitation of and prayer and mourning at the tombs.

32-38 Chapter [Five]. Classification into four groups of souls after death and their corresponding abodes in the period between death and resurrection; reception of the newly deceased by other souls; prohibition of suicide; confrontation of Adam and Moses; the punishment of *barzakh*.

38-44 Chapter [Six]. The trumpet heralds the day of resurrection; cataclysmic events of the Hour; God's manifestation and declaration of sovereignty; the Fire [*saqar*] is drawn forth and repulsed; the dead earth is revived; bodies are resurrected; Isrāfīl's trumpet; the souls united with their bodies wait naked on their graves; the clothing of the dead.

44-46 Chapter [Seven]. The time between the two trumpet blasts; different opinions on the length of that period; the dread of that period.

46-66 Chapter [Eight]. Each person waiting on his grave with his own light before him; the personification of deeds as riding animals; loss of one's sense faculties at the Hour; the materialization of earthly temptations; resurrection of martyrs; the angels of the seven heavens surround the dead in concentric circles; the confusion and perspiring of the dead; children give cups of water to the thirsty; the second blast of the horn and the arrival of the Throne; seeking intercession with God; only the Prophet Muḥammad is fit to intercede; descriptions of the afflictions of the negligent and the profligate.

66-70 Chapter [Nine]. Intercession of the Prophet; arrival of the Garden and the Fire; terror of the assembled at the sight of the Fire; the setting of the balance and judgment of beasts.

70-78 The summoning of the tablet and the messengers with their respective communities to witness to the claims of Gabriel; recitation of the Torah; the Psalms, the Gospel and the Qur'ān by Moses, David, Jesus, and Muḥammad.

78-81 The reckoning of every individual and testimony of the hands and feet; commission of the wrongdoers to *jahannam*.

81-83 The appearance of God to the believers in false and true form; the bridge of Ṣirāṭ; the A^{c}rāf; the Basin and river of Kawthar.

83-88 The distractions of the living from concentration in prayer; repentant sinners; recompense to the blind, the afflicted, the righteous, the lovers of God, those who fear God, and the poor.

89-97 Accusation against the rich, the troubled, the elegant young men and their slaves, and the poor for neglecting God; cases of individual confrontation of God and expressions of God's mercy; condemnation of the taking of life; redemption from the Fire of those who have been temporarily punished.

97-101 The state of transgressors in the Fire; those of the community of Muḥammad who have committed major transgressions in the Fire; mercy for those who have faith and hope in God.

101-109 God rolls up the heavens and the earth; each individual feels alone at judgment; the raining down of the leaves of each individual's book; those who enter the the Garden without reckoning; the messengers and prophets and *ᶜulamā'* on thrones; personification of the Qur'ān, the earth, and Friday.

110 Conclusion.

TRANSLATION OF *AL-DURRA AL-FĀKHIRA*

The Book of the Precious Pearl Concerning the Disclosure of the Sciences of the Hereafter. The composition of the venerable, the Imam, the erudite and most learned, proof of Islam, Abū Ḥāmid Muḥammad b. Muḥammad b. Muḥammad al-Ghazālī al-Ṭūsī, may God sanctify his spirit and illumine his tomb. Amen.

In the name of God, the Merciful, the Beneficent.

Thus said the Shaykh, the Imam, the learned, the proof of Islam, Abū Ḥāmid Muḥammad b. Muḥammad b. Muḥammad al-Ghazālī al-Ṭūsī, may God sanctify and illumine his tomb.[1]

/2/ Praise be to God, Who singled out Himself for eternal existence and ordained mortality for all others. He made death the possession of the people of *kufr* and of *islām*[2] alike; by His knowledge He set down the different categories of judgment; He appointed the hereafter following the allotted days [of a man's life]. All of that He reveals to whomever He wills from among the honored people of His creation. May the blessing of God be upon our lord Muḥammad, Messenger of the omniscient King, and on his family and his companions, on whom He has conferred abundance of favor in the abode of peace.

And now to our subject. Truly, God, exalted be He, says, ⟨Every soul [*nafs*] will taste death...⟩, and that is attested to in His Book in three places,[3] for God, praised be He, and exalted, desired three deaths for the worlds. Thus he who belongs to the earthly world dies, he who belongs to the Malakūtī world dies, and he who belongs to the Jabarūtī world dies.[4] The first refers to Adam and his descendents and all living beings, according to their three species.[5] The Malakūtī or second world contains the various kinds of angels and *jinn*.[6] And the people of the Jabarūtī world are the chosen from among the angels, as God, may He be exalted, said, ⟨God chooses Messengers from among angels and men...⟩ [S 22:75] There are the cherubim [*al-karūbīyūn*], the bearers of the Throne[7] and companions of the pavilions of God the Majestic.[8] God described and extolled them in His Book when He said, ⟨...those who are with Him are neither too proud nor too weary to serve Him; they praise Him night and day, without ceasing.﴿ [S 21:19-20] They are the people of the Holy Presence, as is signified by His saying, ﴾We would have taken it from that which is in Our presence, had We but [wanted to] /3/ do it.﴿ [S 21:17] These die despite their position and proximity to God; for even their rank will not keep them from death.

The first thing I shall mention to you concerns earthly death. If you have faith in God, His Messenger, and the Last Day, open your ears so that you may give heed to what I convey to you. I shall describe it to you as the progression from one state to another. God testifies to what I say and the Qur'ān confirms my speech, as do the sound reports from the Messenger of God.

CHAPTER When God, may He be exalted, gathered up mankind into two groups, He did it by stroking the back of Adam,[9] God's peace be on him. Those that He gathered first He put on the right, and those He gathered the second time He put on the left. Then God spread His two hands to Adam. Adam looked at them and the groups were contained in His two noble palms like atoms. Then He said, "These are destined for the Garden and I am not anxious about them; their activities are those of people of the Garden. And those others are destined for the Fire, and I am not anxious about them either, for their activities are those of people of the Fire." So Adam said, "O Lord, what are the acts of the people of the Garden?" He replied, "Three things: faith in Me, confirmation of My messengers, and following My Book concerning what is commanded and forbidden." "And what," said Adam, "are the acts of the people of the Fire?" God answered, "Three things: association of anything with Me, giving the lie to My messengers, and denying My Book concerning what is commanded and forbidden." So Adam said, "O Lord, let them testify concerning themselves; perhaps they will not do it. ﴾...He caused them to testify concerning themselves, [saying], 'Am I not your

Lord?' /4/ They answered, 'Yes! We do testify!...*
[S 7:172]"[10] He had the angels and Adam testify that they confirmed His lordship. Then He returned them to their place, now living souls without bodies. When He had returned them to the loins of Adam He caused them to die, then seized their souls and placed them near Him in one of the treasurehouses.

When the individual sperm falls, it is established in the womb until its form is completed. The soul in it is lifeless, but its essential Malakūtī nature keeps the body from decomposing. Then God, may He be exalted, breathes into it His spirit, rendering to it its secret essence that had been taken and hidden for a time in one of the treasurehouses of the Throne. The infant gets agitated -- and how many an infant does so in the belly of his mother. Perhaps his mother pays attention to him, or perhaps she does not. This is a first death and a second life.

CHAPTER Then God, may He be exalted, places him in the world for the days of his life until he completes his appointed time[11] and his allotted means of sustenance and all that has been prescribed for him. And when his destiny approaches, that is, his earthly death, then the four angels descend to him: the angel who pulls the soul from his right foot, the angel who pulls it from the left foot, and the angel who pulls it from his right hand, and the angel who pulls it from his left hand. Some of the circumstances of the Malakūtī world may be unveiled to the dying person before he expires so that he sees those angels, not the way they actually appear in their own world, but according to the extent of his understanding. If his tongue is unhampered he may tell about their existence or the existence of others like him. Perhaps he talks to /5/ himself about what he saw, and one thinks that it is due to the workings of Satan on him. Then he is silent so that his tongue is tied, while they pull the soul from the tips of his fingers. The good soul slips out like the jetting of water from a water-skin, but the profligate's spirit [*rūḥ*][12] squeaks out like a skewer from wet wool.

Thus the giver of the law, Muḥammad, on whom be God's blessing and peace,[13] has related, "The dead person imagines that his belly is filled with thorns; it seems as if his soul is squeezed out through the eye of a needle, and as if the sky is pressed down on the earth and he is between them." In this connection, Kaᶜb al-Aḥbār [14] was asked about death, and he replied, "It is as if a thorny branch were placed in a man's abdomen, and a strong person pulled it out, breaking off what he could break and letting the rest remain." The Prophet also said that one death agony is stronger than three hundred blows from a sword. When it occurs, one's forehead sweats, his eyes see falsely, his chest lifts up, his soul heaves and he turns a yellow color. When ᶜĀ'isha [15] saw the Messenger of God in this condition, and he was lying on her lap, she recited these verses, choking back her tears: /6/

> By my life, would that I were your ransom from what oppresses you
> In the way of torment, and from what pains you!
> Never did a spirit of madness touch you 'ere this
> Nor were you one to be overawed with terror.
> Why is it that I look into your face
> Seeing it like dye fresh-steeped?

Thus there appear the afflictions of the soul, changing one's face at the moment of death because of the magnitude of the sufferings one undergoes. Then his soul is confined to his heart, and his tongue becomes silent, uttering nothing. No one can speak while the soul is gathered together in his chest because of two mysteries. The first is that the matter is too great for him, for the chest presses upon the soul confined in it. Have you not noticed that when one is hit by a blow on the chest, he remains stunned and unable to speak? Anyone who is stabbed cries out when struck, except the person /7/ stabbed in the chest; he falls down without crying out.

As for the second mystery, it is due to the fact that the movement of the voice comes from the bursting forth of natural heat. When one becomes rigid and stays without moving, he comes to the point where he cannot breathe except with waning force, dissociated from the brain. His soul becomes changed due to two circumstances, elevation and cold, because he has lost his heat.

At this point, the conditions of the dead differ. Some of them are stabbed at that time by an angel with a poisoned sword dipped in a poison of fire. The soul flees, escaping in a stream, and when the angel takes it in his hand it shudders like quicksilver. It is only the size of a bee, but with human characteristics. Then the guardians of hell [*al-zabānīya*][16] take it away.

For some of the dead, the soul is pulled out slowly and gradually to the point where it is confined in the windpipe. But only a small part of it remains in the windpipe, connected to the heart, so at this time the angel pierces it with that sword already described. The soul does not finally separate from the heart until it has been pierced. /8/ The principle of the sword is that it has been dipped in the sea of death. When it is placed in contact with the heart, its principle courses through the body like steeped poison. This is so because the principle of life is situated in the heart where it has exercised its effect from the moment of the first birth.

Some of the theologians have said that life is not identical with the soul, meaning that it is a combination of soul and body.

When the soul has thus risen to the upper part of the body, temptations are presented to it. For instance Iblīs[17] may send his servants to a particular person, placing them over him and putting him in their charge. They come to him while he is in that condition and show him the image of someone who has died before him, of those whom he loved, and who gave him counsel in the abode of this world, such as his father, mother, brother sister or intimate friend. They say to him, "You are dying, O Fulān,[18] and we have gone before you in this matter. Die as a Jew for it is the religion acceptable to God." And if he turns away from them and refuses, others come and say to him, "Die as a Christian, for it is the religion of the Messiah,[19] and by it is abrogated /9/ the religion of Moses." Then they mention to him the articles of faith of each religion.

It is at that point that God turns aside all of those for whom He wills deviation. That is the meaning of His word, ❨Our Lord! do not cause our hearts to deviate after You have guided us, but from Your Presence grant us mercy. Truly You are the Bounteous Giver.❩ [S 3:8] That is, do not make our hearts deviate when You have guided us prior to that time.

When God wants to acknowledge and guide His servant, He sends to him the angel of mercy, and it is said that that is Gabriel [Jibrīl].[20] He drives the demons away from the dying person, so that the pallor is removed from his face and he actually smiles. Most of those seen smiling in this situation are joyful because of the envoy who brings mercy from God, saying, "O Fulān, do you not know me? I am Gabriel, and those are your enemies from among the demons. Die in the religion of the pious monotheists [*al-milla al-ḥanīfīya*] and the way of Muḥammad [*al-sharīʿa al-Muḥammadīya*]. Nothing is more beloved to a person nor more joyous to him than that." And this is His word, ❨...from Your Presence grant us mercy. Truly You are the Bounteous Giver.❩ [S 3:8].

Then the dead person is taken at the time when the angel pierces him. One may be pierced while he is at prayer, or /10/ sleeping, or going about some business of his, or intent on amusement. It comes as a surprise, for the soul is seized but one time. Then there is also the one who, when his soul reaches his throat, sees unveiled for him his kin who have preceeded him, and is surrounded by his neighbors from the dead.[21] He utters a kind of lowing which all creatures save man can hear; if man hears it he is struck senseless.

The last faculty lost to the dying person is that of hearing. When the connection between the spirit and the heart is broken, sight is destroyed, but hearing is not lost until the soul is seized. Thus Muḥammad, on whom be God's blessing and peace, said, "Recite to your dying the testimony that there is no God but God." But he forbade them to repeat it too often because the dying at that moment are experiencing the greatest terror and mortal apprehension.

When you look at the dying person and his mouth waters, his lips contract, his face turns black and his eyes become bluish, then know that he is miserable. The reality of his wretchedness in the hereafter has been unveiled to him. And when you see the dying person and his mouth is hollow as if he were laughing, his face beaming, his eyes cast down, then know that he has been told the good news of the joy that will come to him in the hereafter; /11/ the reality of his blessedness has been revealed to him.

When the angel seizes the happy soul, two angels with beautiful faces, wearing lovely clothes and with sweet-smelling fragrance, take it and wrap it in silk taken from the silk of the Garden. The soul is the size of a bee, with human characteristics, and has not lost its intelligence or its knowledge acquired in this world. They ascend with it in the air, and continue to pass by former communities and past eras, much like swarms of locusts scattered about. Among them are some whom he knows, and others whom he does not know. Finally they arrive at the near heaven [*samā' al-dunyā*] and al-Amīn[22] [Gabriel] knocks at the gate. Then a voice says to al-Amīn, "Who are you?" He answers, "I am Ṣalṣā'īl[23] and this is /12/ Fulān with me," using the most excellent and the most beloved of his names. The reply comes, "Yes, the man was Fulān, and there is no doubt that his faith was sound." Then they reach the second heaven and al-Amīn knocks at the gate. "Who are you?" Gabriel says what he said the first time. And the reply comes, "Welcome to Fulān! He used to observe his prayers on all the occasions requiring them."

Then they pass until they reach the third heaven. Al-Amīn knocks at the door, and a voice says, "Who are you?" He repeats what he said the first time, and they hear, "Greetings to Fulān. He used to honor God in respect to his possessions and not cling to any of them." Again they move on until they reach the fourth heaven, and he knocks on the gate. "Who are you?" comes the question, and al-Amīn repeats the same speech again. Then comes the response, "Welcome to Fulān. He used to fast and he did it well, refraining from using obscenity or eating forbidden food." Again they pass until they reach /13/ the fifth heaven. He knocks on the door and when "Who are you?" comes, he responds again with the usual answer. Then they hear, "Welcome to Fulān. He performed the pilgimage required by God, without pretention or hypocrisy."[24]

Continuing on, they reach the sixth heaven and he knocks on the gate. "Who are you?" Al-Amīn answers as is his habit. "Greetings," comes the reply, "to the righteous man and the good soul. He used to have great piety toward his parents." The gate is opened for him, and they pass on until they reach the seventh heaven. Gabriel knocks on the door, and they hear, "Who are you?"

Al-Amīn says his usual speech, to which is said, "Greetings to Fulān. He used to seek God's forgiveness until the morning and to give alms in secret and to provide for orphans." The gate opens for them and they pass on until they reach the majestic pavilions. There he knocks on the door and again hears the question, "Who are you?" Al-Amīn gives his usual reply, and the response comes, "Welcome to the worthy servant and the noble soul. He used to ask forgiveness often, commanding that which is good, forbidding /14/ the reprehensible and showing generosity to the poor."

Then they pass by a group of angels, all of them giving good tidings to the soul and greeting him, until they arrive at the Lote-tree of the boundary.[25] Gabriel knocks at the door, and a voice says, "Who are you?" Al-Amīn responds in the usual way, to which is said, "Welcome to Fulān. His deeds were righteous in the eyes of God." The gate is opened for them and they pass respectively through oceans of fire, light, darkness, water, ice and hail. The length of each of these oceans is one thousand years. Then they penetrate the coverings affixed to the Throne of Mercy. There are eighty thousand balconies and each balcony having a moon radiant upon God, glorifying Him and venerating Him. If one of these moons should appear in the near heaven, it would be worshipped instead of God and its light would singe the earth.

Then a herald from /15/ the Holy Presence calls from behind those pavilions, "Who is this soul whom you have brought?" "Fulān ibn Fulān," he replies. Then the Glorious One says, "Let him approach. Truly you are an excellent servant, O My servant." He stops him in front of Him, embarrassing him with some rebuke and reproof until the soul thinks that he is doomed. Then He pardons him, may He be glorified and exalted.

There is a story about Yaḥyá ibn Aktham al-Qāḍī,[26] who was seen in a dream.[27] He was asked, "What did God do to you?" and he replied, "He made me stop in front of Him, then He said to me, "Oh you evil old man, you have done this and that.' I said, 'O Lord, what about that which has been told to me about You?' God said, 'And what have you been told about Me, O Yaḥyá?' I answered, 'My God and my Lord, Muᶜammar told me from al-Zuhrī[28] from ᶜUrwa[29] from ᶜĀ'isha who was told it from the Prophet, from Gabriel, from You, may You be glorified, that You said: I am reluctant to /16/ punish an old person who has matured in Islam.' Then He smiled and said, 'O Yaḥyá, you are right, as were Muᶜammar and al-Zuhrī and ᶜUrwah. And ᶜĀ'isha was right and Muḥammad and Gabriel. I spoke the truth; go, for I have pardoned you.'"

Ibn Nubāta[30] was also seen in a dream and he was asked, "What did God do to you?" He answered, "He made me stop before Him, saying, 'You are the one whose speech is so pure that people say, How eloquent he is!' But I replied, 'Glory be to you! I was describing You!' Then He said, 'Speak as you used to speak in the earthly world.' So I said, 'He Who created them has destroyed them; He Who made them speak has silenced them; He Who brought them into being has annihilated them. And as He destroyed them, so will He again bring them into being; as He created them, so will He return them and restore them.' So God said to me, 'You are correct. Go, for I forgive you.'"

The story is also told about Manṣūr ibn ᶜAmmār,[31] who was seen in a dream and was asked, "What did God do to you?" He replied, "He made me stop in front of Him and He said to me, 'What have you brought to Me, O Manṣūr?' I said, 'Thirty-six pilgrimages.' He answered, 'I do not accept any one of them.' Then He said, 'What else have you brought me, O Manṣūr?' 'Three hundred and sixty recitations of the Qur'ān,' I said. He told me, 'I do not accept any one of them.' Then He said /17/ to me, 'What have you brought to Me, O Manṣūr?' 'The fasts of sixty years,' said I. 'I do not accept one of them,' came the answer. 'What have you brought to me, O Manṣūr?' I then replied, 'I have brought to You Yourself!' And He said to me, Glory be to Him, 'Now you have come unto Me. Go, for I forgive you.'"

There are many stories related of these matters. I have told you somewhat of them, that he who is to be guided may be guided by them; God is the One to Whom we turn for assistance.

There are some people who, upon finally reaching the Throne, hear the cry, "Send him back!" Then there are some who are thrust back from the veils of the Throne. Only those who know God reach Him, and only the people of the fourth station[32] and beyond actually stand before Him.

CHAPTER As for the profligate, his soul is taken harshly, his face like the one who eats colocynth. The angel says, "Go away from me, oh you evil soul of noxious body!" Then he shrieks louder than the braying of a donkey. When ʿIzrā'īl[33] seizes his soul he delivers it to the guardians of hell, who have repulsive faces, black clothes and rotten breath, and hold in their hands a hair shirt in which they wrap the soul.[34] The human person is changed into one the size of a locust. The unbeliever is larger in size than the believer; I refer, of course, to the Hereafter. And in truth, the *kāfir* in the Fire is like the Mount of Uḥud.[35]

The angel ascends with the soul until they reach the gate of the near heaven, and al-Amīn knocks at the door. A voice says, "Who are you?" and he replies, "I am Daqyā'īl" because the name of the angel responsible to /18/ the myrmidons of punishment is Daqyā'īl. Then he is asked, "Who is with you?" to which he replies, Fulān ibn Fulān," using the ugliest and most loathsome of the names he had in the earthly realm. Then he is told, "You are not welcome!" ﴾...and the gates of heaven are not opened to them, and they do not enter the Garden.﴿ [S 7:40]

When al-Amīn hears this speech, he flings the soul from his hands, and the wind drops it in a far distant place. That accords with His word, ﴾...For whoever ascribes partners to God, it is as if he fell from the sky and a bird carried him away or the wind descended on him [and deposited him] in a distant place.﴿ [S 22:31] Oh what a disgrace has befallen him! And when he reaches the earth, the guardians of hell rush to him and lead him to Sijjīn,[36] a huge stone to which are brought immoral spirits.

As for the Christians and the Jews, they return from the Throne to their graves. This is for those who followed their faith, and each observes his washing and his burial. The one who ascribes partners to God, however, does not witness that, because he has been dropped [by the wind]. And as for the hypocrite, he is like the one who is sent back to his grave, odious and banished.

The negligent among the believers are of different kinds. First is the worshipper whose prayer is refused because he was negligent in its performance, taking only little time for it. /19/ The prayer is rolled up just as shabby clothes are rolled up, and the servant's face is struck with it. Then the prayer ascends, saying, "May God neglect you as you have neglected me!"

Then there is the one whose alms are returned because he gave them only so that it could be said, "How charitable Fulān is!" Perhaps he even gave out alms in the presence of women in the attempt to win their affection. We have seen instances of this, may God preserve us from such a thing!

Another type is the one whose fast is rejected because while fasting from food he did not abstain from obscene and depraved speech. The month of fasting turns away from him, because he has falsified it.

There is also the person whose pilgrimage is returned to him because he only performed it so that it might be said, "Fulān has made the pilgrimage!", or it may be he made the pilgrimage with ill-earned gains.

Among those who are rejected is the person refractory to his parents. Other concerns of piety are known only to those learned in the secrets of good conduct and sincerity of actions performed for the King, the Benevolent.

And all of this is what is meant by the various traditions and narratives, such as that /20/ related by Muᶜādh ibn Jabal[37] about the rejection of deeds, and other such things. I only wish to suggest the matter here, for volumes have been filled in confirmation of it, and people knowledgeable in the law [*al-sharᶜ*] know the truth of these matters as well as they know their own children.

When the soul is returned to the body, it finds it has already been taken for the washing, if it is to be washed. So it sits near the head until the body is washed. God opens up the vision of those among the righteous whom He wills, so that they can see the soul in its earthly form. Thus a man related that he washed one of his sons, when suddenly he materialized, sitting near the head of the body. Fear overcame him, so he left the side from which he saw the figure and turned to the other side. The figure continued to watch until the dead body was encased in his winding sheets, then it returned to its shroud. Also the learned man saw him on the bier.[38]

Thus it has been related on the authority of more than one pious person that [the Prophet] ordered them to call out over the bier, "Where is Fulān? Where is the spirit [*al-rūḥ*]?" /21/ and the shroud trembled spontaneously two or three times.

Rabīʿ ibn Khaytham[39] has told about one dead person who became agitated in the hands of his washer. He spoke on his bier about the era of Abū Bakr al-Ṣiddīq mentionin his excellence [*faḍl*] and that of ʿUmar al-Fārūq.[40] He then concluded by mentioning the virtues of ʿUthmān. Truly this soul had witnessed Malakūtī matters; God opens up the hearing of whomever of His creation He wishes.

When the dead person has been wrapped in his winding-clothes, his soul becomes attached to the chest on the outside, lowing and crying and saying, "Hurry with me to whatever mercy you are taking me, if indeed you know what it is!" And if it has been informed of its misfortune, it says, "Slowly, slowly to whatever punishment you are taking me, if in fact you know what it is!" For that reason the Messenger of God did not allow a funeral procession /22/ to pass without standing as it went by. In the Ṣaḥīḥ it says that a funeral procession passed before him and he stood in salutation. So someone said to him, "O Messenger of God, he is a Jew." The Prophet replied, "Was he not a soul?" He used to do this because the Malakūtī secrets were unveiled to him; he took pleasure in death when it passed by him, for he was one of those who understood its meaning.

When the dead person is put into his grave and the earth is poured on him, the grave calls to him, "You used to enjoy yourself on my surface, but now you will grieve in my interior; you used to eat all kinds of delicacies on my surface, but today the worms will eat you while your are inside me."[41] It repeats to him many similar expressions of rebuke until the dirt is leveled over him. Then an angel whose name is Rūmān[42] calls to him. It is related that Ibn Masᶜūd[43] once told how he had asked, "O Messenger of God, what is the first thing the dead person encounters when he is put in his grave?" And he replied, "O Ibn Masᶜūd, you are asking me about something no one else has asked about. The first thing that happens is that the angel Rūmān comes, roaming about the graves and saying, 'O servant of God, write down your deeds.' And he answers, 'I do not have any ink or paper.' So Rūmān says, 'You are wrong! Your shroud is your paper, your saliva your ink and your finger your pen.' So he cuts for him a piece of his shroud, and makes the servant write, even if he could not write /23/ while in this world. He mentions then his good and bad deeds as if it were a question of only one day. Then the angel folds up the piece of shroud and fastens it on his neck." At that point the Messenger of God recited, ⁅We have fastened the fate of every man on his neck...⁆ [S 17:13], referring to his deeds.

When that is concluded, the two interrogators of the grave enter.[44] They are two black angels who rend apart the earth with their fangs. They have their hair down dragging the ground. Their voices are like cracking thunder, their eyes like flashing lightning and their breath like a violent wind. In the hand of each one of them is an iron rod so heavy that the inhabitants of heaven and earth together could not lift it. If the largest mountain were hit by it, it would be destroyed. Seeing them, the soul shudders and flies away, entering into the nostrils of the dead person. Life is revived in his breast, and he then has a form such as he had at the time when the death agony came. He cannot move although he hears and sees.

The angels interrogate him with severity and reproach him with roughness. Suddenly the dusty earth becomes /24/ like water to him wherein he moves freely, and finds pleasureful relief. Then they say to him, "Who is your Lord, and what is you religion [*dīn*], and who is your Prophet, and what is your prayer direction [*qibla*]?" God determines a sure and right response for those for whom He assures success, so that his response [to the question of the angels] is, "He Who gave you authority and He Who sent you to me." This is said only by the virtuous *ᶜulamā'*.[45] At this one of the angels says to the other, "He is correct; we have chastised him sufficiently." Then they expand the top of the tomb for him like a great dome, and open for him a gate to the Garden opposite his right side. They spread out for him some of its silks and perfumes, and refreshing breezes from the Garden waft in to him.[46] His good deeds come to him in the form of the loveliest of creatures,[47] putting him at ease and talking to him while his grave is filled with light. He rejoices without ceasing and is full of bliss for as long as he remains on the earth, until the Hour[48] comes. Yet he continues to ask, "When will the Hour arrive?", for there is nothing he would like better than its coming.

Below him in rank is the believer who did good works but had no portion of religious knowledge or of the /25/ secrets of the Malakūt. His deeds enter in the best of forms with pleasant perfume and attractive clothing, saying to him,"Do you not know me?" And he replies, "Who are you, whom God has graced me with in my exile?" The figure says, "I am your own good deeds, so do not grieve and do not be afraid; very soon Munkar and Nakīr will enter and question you, so do not be taken back." Then it instructs him about his defense. While he is at this, the two angels enter, as was described above. They chide him with angry words and make him sit down, supported on his back. Then they say to him, "Who is your Lord...?" as was done before. He answers in a clear voice, "God is my Lord and Muḥammad is my Prophet and the Qur'ān is my guide, and Islam is my religion and the Kaᶜba is my prayer direction and Abraham is my father and his community [*milla*] is my community." Then they say to him, "You are correct," and they do with him as was described in the first case, except that they open for him a door to the Fire on his left side. He gazes at its serpents and scorpions and chains and fetters and boiling water and [the tree of] Zaqqūm[49] and its festering matter and all its affliction, and he is miserable. Then they say to him, "That misfortune is not for you; God has exchanged your place on the Fire for a place in the Garden; sleep in peace." They shut the door to the Fire and open for him the door to the Garden, and he is unaware of the passing /26/ of the months and years and ages.

Then there is the one whose responses are obscure. If his real creed was something different [from what is commanded], it is impossible for him to say, "God is my Lord," and he mumbles something else. So they strike him such a blow that the grave is set on fire. It dies down for awhile, then it begins to burn again, and this is his situation as long as he remains in the earth. There is also the person for whom it is extremely difficult to say, "Islam is my religion," because he may have experienced doubt or succumbed to a temptation at the time of death. So they strike him a single blow and his tomb is set ablaze with fire, like the one before. Still another finds it difficult to say, "The Qur'ān is my guide," for though he used to read it, he did not accept its admonition, nor did he carry out its commands or refrain from that which it forbids. He devoted time to it, but his soul did not profit from it. And so he is treated as are the others.

There is another whose deeds are transformed into a young dog that punishes him in the grave according to the degree of his sin, or into a piglet, son of a swine. For some it is difficult to say, "Muḥammad is my Prophet", because they were forgetful of his way [*sunna*]. Another cannot utter, "The Kaᶜba is my prayer direction", because he attended it so little in his prayer or was imperfect in his ablutions, or turned around while /27/ praying so that his prayer postures and prostrations were incorrect. What has been reported concerning those things that are virtuous in prayer suffices to let you know that God does not accept prayer from one who is negligent or wears forbidden dress.

There is also the kind of person for whom it is difficult to say, "Abraham is my father", because one day he heard something that made him fear that Abraham was a Jew or a Christian, filling him with doubt. So what is done to the others is done to him. And all of these various kinds of people we have already discussed in the Kitāb al-Iḥyā'.[50]

CHAPTER As for the profligate, the two angels said to him, "Who is your Lord?" and he replies, "I do not know." So they say to him, "You do not know and are not aware?" Then they strike him with those iron rods until he is beaten down to the seventh earth. Then the earth casts him back into his grave, and they hit him seven times more.

There are a variety of circumstances for the profligates. The works of some are changed into dogs snapping at them until the Hour arrives; these are the rebels. Those of others are changed into swine by which they are tormented in the grave; these are the skeptics. Such are some of the conditions into which the inhabitants of the graves fall, which we have mentioned only in abbreviated form. The reason for the variation is that the individual is only punished in his grave by something that he feared on earth. Some people fear dogs more than lions, for the natures of created beings /28/ differ. We ask peace and pardon from God before we have cause for remorse.

The story is told that someone who had died was seen in a dream and was asked, "How are you?" He replied, "I prayed one day without performing the ablutions, so God put a wolf in charge of me to frighten me in my grave. My situation with him is a most terrible one!" Another was seen in a dream and was asked, "What did God do with you?" He answered, "Leave me alone! One day I did not perform the ablution for ritual impurity, so God dressed me in a robe of fire in which I writhe." Another was seen and was asked about what God had done to him, and he said, "The washer who washed me [at death] handled me roughly, lacerating me on a nail sticking out of the washingroom, and I have suffered from it." When morning came the washer was questioned and he said, "I did not mean to do it." Still another was seen in a dream and was asked, "How are you? Are you not dead?" "Yes," he said, "and I am well except that a stone broke my rib when the earth was levelled over me and it injured me." So the grave was opened and they found him just as he had said.

/29/ Another came to his son while he was sleeping and he said, "O my son, repair the place where your father sleeps, for the rain has damaged it." So when morning came he sent someone to his father's grave and he found that a little stream of water had come upon it from a river and the tomb was filled with water. Then there was the Bedouin who said to his [dead] father, "What did God do to you?" The father replied, "He did not harm me except that I was buried opposite Fulān and he was a sinner. I have been horrified by the different torments he received!"

Much of what is found in stories like these explains that the dead are tormented in their graves. Sufficient as an indication is the narrative in which the Master of the Law [Muḥammad] says, "The dead is pained in his grave by the same things that pain a living man." The Messenger of God forbade breaking the bones of the dead. He once passed by a man sitting in front of a grave, and told him to stop it, "Do not do harm to the dead in their graves."

Once when the Prophet visited the grave of his mother Āmina, he wept, and it made those with him weep. Then he said, "I asked my Lord permission to pray for pardon for her, and He did not grant it. Then I asked permission to visit her grave, and He granted it to me. /30/ So visit the tombs, for they will make you remember death." Whenever he came to visit the cemetery, he used to say, "Peace be upon the people of these abodes who are among the believing Muslims. Truly if God wills it, we are coming after you. You preceded us and we will follow you. O God, forgive us and them, and by Your Grace refrain from [punishing] us and them." The Prophet used to instruct his wives when the women went out to the cemetery, saying to them, "Say these words," and this was the formula He taught them.

Ṣāliḥ al-Muzannī said, "I asked one of the *ᶜulamā'* why he forbade prayer in the cemetery. He took as his guide a *ḥadīth* [which says], "Do not pray among the graves, because that is an affliction which has no limit." Another has related, "I was praying one day in the cemetery when the heat became intense; then I saw someone who looked like my father on the back of his grave. I prostrated myself in terror and I heard him saying, 'The earth is too confined for you, so you had to come annoying us after some time with your prayer!"

In a narrative of the Ṣaḥīḥ it says that the Messenger of God, passing by an orphan crying at the grave of his father, wept out of compassion for him. Then he said, "Indeed the dead person is tormented by the tears of the living over him."[51] That is, he is grieved and afflicted by them. How many of the dead seen in dreams, when asked, "How are you, O Fulān?" reply /31/ "My condition is poor because of Fulān and Fulāna, who are shedding many tears over me." (The Zindīqs,[52] however, deny that.)

The Ṣaḥīḥ relates that the Messenger of God said, "No one of you passes by the grave of his brother Muslim whom he knew on the earth and gives him peace but that the dead person recognizes him and returns peace to him." In the same way, while he was turning away from a bier that had just been buried, he said, "He hears the thumpings of your sandals, and if he hears that, he is even better able to hear other things."

One of the dervishes [*faqīr*s] died before he had made his testament. So he began to rove about his house at night, saying, "Give to Fulān such and such a portion of crops, and return to Fulān his book which I had with me for some time." And when morning came each [of the dervishes] mentioned to the other what he had seen. Then they gave the crops, but though they searched for the book they did not find it. This surprised them greatly, but then after some time they found it in a corner of the house.

Someone else has related this story: "Our father engaged for us a teacher to teach us our lessons at home. Then the teacher died. After six days we went to his grave to visit him, /32/ and began to discuss with each other the matter of God's command, may He be exalted. Someone passed by us selling a plate of figs, which we bought and ate, throwing the stems onto the grave. When night came, the Shaykh saw the dead man in a dream, and said to him, 'How are you?' 'Fine,' he replied, 'except that your children took my grave for a garbage pile and talked about me, with words that are nothing but infidelity!" The Shakyh reprimanded us, and we said [to each other], 'Glory be to God! He continues to bother us in the hereafter just as he did on the earth!'"

There are many of these stories. I have mentioned only these few examples, and as admonitions, so that the many might be considered on the basis of the few.

CHAPTER As for the people of the tombs, they are to be found in four conditions: First there are those who remain on their shoulders until /33/ their individuality[53] fades away, their corpses become bloated and their bodies return to dust. Then they continue to wander around the realm below the earthly heaven.

Next are the ones whom God allows to slumber, so that they do not know what has happened to them until they are awakened with the first blast [of the trumpet]; then they die. Then there are those who only stay in their graves for two or three months, after which their souls mount on birds which fly with them up to the Garden. A sound *ḥadīth* relates that the Master of the Law, Muḥammad, said, "The soul of the believer is a bird perched on the trees of the Garden." The true meaning of this is that when he was asked about the spirits [*arwāḥ*] of martyrs, he said, "The spirits of the martyrs are in the crops of green birds perched on the trees of the Garden."[54] Some, when their individuality fades away, rise up to where the trumpet [is to be blown] and remain there until its blast is sounded.

The fourth group is reserved for the prophets [*anbiyā'*] and saints [*awliyā'*]; they have a choice. Some of them choose to remain on the earth, walking about until the Hour comes. Many of them are seen in dreams; I am thinking of al-Ṣiddīq and al-Fārūq[55] in particular. The Prophet himself had the choice of circling through the three worlds. Concerning this choice he said one day, by way of information and instruction, "Truly God prizes me more than that He would leave me in /34/ the earth more than three..." And this was three decades, because Ḥusayn[56] was killed at the beginning of the thirtieth year and the Prophet, angered with the people of the earth, ascended into the sky. One of the pious saw him in a dream and said, "O Messenger of God, dearer to me than my father and my mother! What think you of the strife of your community?" And he replied, "God increases their strife! They murdered Ḥusayn, and did not keep me there!" Then he began to speak a number of words ambiguous to the narrator.

Some of the fourth group, such as Abraham, choose the seventh heaven. In the *ḥadīth* it says that the Prophet passed by him[57] while he was leaning against the Bayt al-Maᶜmūr,[58] surrounded by the children of Muslims. Jesus [ᶜĪsá] is in the fifth heaven. In every heaven are messengers and prophets who remain there and do not leave until the bolt shall fall. Only five among them have a choice: the Friend [al-Khalīl], the Spokesman [al-Kalīm], the Spirit [al-Rūḥ], the Chosen [al-Ṣafīy], and the Beloved [al-Ḥabīb].[59] These end up wherever they wish in the several worlds. As for the friends of God (the saints), some of them are stayed for the earthly resurrection; it was related of Abū Yazīd[60] that he is at the foot of the Throne eating at a table.

Thus in these four kinds of conditions the people of the grave are given punishment, mercy, ease and honor respectively.

Those of them who are on the earth crowd around the dead person when he dies so that the roominess of his abode becomes straitened by them. In some cases they will be visible to the dead and he will see them /35/ and understand who they are. I myself have beheld many who spoke in this fashion. Once I saw one of my friends whose sight was uncovered; he gazed at his son, who was dead, but had penetrated into the house, and was fully conscious and formed. These advantages of the Malakūtī world are only for [those of] a generous or noble nature. We beseech God to grant us of His knowledge that which will immerse us in the ocean of His secrets, so that doubt and uncertainty may pass away.

Among these various kinds of the dead described, none perceives the revolution of night and day except those whose individuality remains and who do not ascend on high. Some of these even recognize Friday and the feast days. When one of the [newly] dead leaves the earth, they all gather around him and recognize who he is. This one may inquire about his wife, another about his son, another about his father, each one asking about his own concerns.[61]

Sometimes someone dies and does not meet any of his acquaintances. This is because something caused him to deviate at the moment of death /36/ so that he died a Jew or a Christian; and he thus goes to join their ranks. Then when someone else from the world arrives, his neighbors ask him, "What do you know about Fulān [the one who converted]?" "He has died." They answer, "Truly we are God's and to Him we return! He has been sent down to the community of the pit [*hāwiya*]."[62]

One person was seen in a dream and was asked, "What did God do to you?" He answered, "I am with Fulān and Fulān" (numbering five of his companions), "in excellence and wellbeing." He and his five companions had been slain by the Khārijites.[63] Then he was asked concerning a neighbor of his, "What has God done with him?" and he said, "We have not seen him." The one mentioned had thrown himself into the sea, so that he drowned. I believe - though God knows best - that he is with those who take their own lives.

The Ṣaḥīḥ relates that the Messenger of God once said, "Whoever kills himself with a sharp knife will be found on the day of resurrection with it in his hand, stabbing himself in the belly in the fire of Hell [*jahannam*], where he will remain eternally. Thus the one who kills himself continues in the condition in which he died. Whoever purposefully falls off a mountain and kills himself falls on his skull in the fire of Hell, just as a woman who dies during legal punishment continues to feel the pain until the trumpet blast. And that is the second /37/ life.

It is related on sound authority that Adam met Moses, and Moses said to him, "You are the one whom God created by His hand and in whom He breathed His spirit. His angels prostrated themselves before you, and He allowed you to dwell in His Garden.[64] So why did you renounce him?" Adam replied, "O Moses, you are the one to whom God gave His word, revealing to you the Torah. Have you not seen in it the words, 'And Adam disobeyed His Lord'?" Moses said to him, "Yes." And Adam continued, "For how many years before I committed the sin had it been ordained for me?" "It was decreed for you fifty thousand years before you committed it," said Moses, to which Adam replied, "So then, O Moses, do you blame me for a sin ordained for me fifty thousand years before its commission?"

In the Ṣaḥīḥ it says that the Messenger of God prayed with the messengers on the night of his ascent, prostrating himself two times, and that he invoked the peace of Aaron [Hārūn] and prayed for mercy on him and his community, and that he did the same for Enoch [Idrīs]. Those two had died, and their individuality had disappeared. This is only the life of the soul, and it is after the resurrection that the second life comes. The first life began with the day in which ﴾...He made them testify concerning themselves, "Am I not your Lord?" They answered, "Yes! We do testify!"...﴿ [S 7:172].[65] The earthly life cannot be counted, for it is only a mockery of contentment. Concerning this it is related that the Prophet said, "Mankind is asleep; and when people die, they awaken."

Such are the conditions of the dead. When their individuality disappears from them some are stationary, /38/ some move around, some are stricken and others are punished. The truth of that is illustrated by His having said, ❁They will be brought in front of the Fire morning and evening, and on the day that the Hour arrives, the people of Pharaoh will be made to enter the greatest punishment.❁ [S 40:46] "The day" is proof of the punishment of *barzakh*.[66]

CHAPTER When God so wills it, the blowing of the trumpet will usher in the arrival of the Hour, according to the mysteries which we have described in the Iḥyā'. Then the mountains will be scattered and will move like the clouds; the seas will gush forth one into the other and the sun will be rolled up and will return to black ashes; the oceans will overflow until the atmosphere is filled up with water. The worlds will pass into each other, the stars will fall like a broken string of pearls and the sky will become like rose balm, rotating like a turning /39/ millstone. The earth will shake with a tremendous shaking, sometimes contracting and sometimes expanding like a skin until God orders the stripping of the spheres. In all of the seven earths and the seven heavens, as well as the vicinity of the Throne, no living being will remain, their souls all having departed. Even if one is spiritual, his spirit will depart.[67] The earth will be empty of its inhabitants and the sky of its dwellers, including all of the various species of creatures.

Then God will manifest Himself in the clouds, seizing the seven heavens in His right hand and the seven earths in His left, saying, "O world, O worldly one! Where are your masters? Where are your chiefs? You have beguiled them with your splendors and with your beauty you have kept them from concern for things of the hereafter." Then He extols His own praise as He so desires; He glorifies His eternal existence and His lasting power and never-ending dominion and victorious omnipotence and boundless wisdom. Three times He asks, "To Whom belongs the Kingdom this day?" No one answers Him so He answers Himself, saying, "To God Who is One alone, victorious!"

Then He does something even more awesome; taking the heavens on one finger and the earths on another finger /40/ He twirls them around, saying, "I am the King! I am the King! Where are those who worship other than Me, apart from Me, ascribing partners to Me, while yet partaking of My sustenance? Where are those who found the power to do evil through the comforts I have provided them? Where are the tyrants? Where are the ones who were haughty and proud? To Whom belongs the kingdom today if not to Me!"

Thus He remains, may He be glorified and exalted, for as long as He wishes. From the Throne to the sea[68] not a rational living creature remains, and God deafens the ears of the *hūr* and the beautiful young men [*wuldān*] in the Garden.[69]

Then God opens up a well-spring in Hell [*saqar*] and tongues of flame leap out of it, igniting the fourteen seas as if they were fluffy wool, so that not a single drop remains. The earths become like black charcoal and the heavens like turbid oil or molten copper. But just when the flames are about to engulf the visible parts of the sky, God drives back the fire with one stroke; the flames die down for a thousand years and do not rise up again.

Finally God opens one of the treasurehouses of the Throne in which is contained the sea of life. He causes it to rain upon the earth; it is like male sperm falling upon the parched, dead and barren ground, /41/ which then begins to quiver with life.[70] The rain continues to fall until it covers the entire earth, and the water upon it is four cubits deep.

At that point each body begins to grow from the coccyx [*al-ʿuṣʿuṣ*]. There is a tradition which says that man begins from the tail bone and from it he also will return.[71] Another version says that man disintegrates completely except for the tail bone; from it he begins and from it he will return. This is a bone corresponding to a chickpea in size, with no marrow. From it the bodies grow in their graves just as plants grow, until they become intertwined with each other -- this head on those shoulders, this arm on that side and this thigh on that rump. This is because of the great number of people and it is the meaning of His having said, ﴾We know how much of them the earth takes away, for with Us is a well-guarded Book.﴿ [S 50:4] In this is a great mystery which we have noted in our book al-Iḥyā'. When the re-formation is completed, each person is as he used to be: the boy is a boy, the old man is an old man, the adult is an adult, the youth is a youth, and the young man is a young man.

The Glorious one, glorified be His majesty, orders from under the Throne a rushing wind, in which there is an ethereal fire. By it the earth is stripped, so that no elevation and no undulation and no curvature remain. The mountains are returned to sand like a level dune.

Then God raises to life /42/ Isrāfīl,[72] who blows the trumpet on the rock of Bayt al-Maqdis.[73] The horn is composed of forty circles of light, each circle like the circumference of the sky and the earth. In it are holes equal to the number of created spirits; the spirits go out with a drone like the droning of bees, filling the entire space from the East to the West. Then with God's guiding inspiration every soul goes to its body, the beast and the bird and all those creatures having a spirit [*rūḥ*].[74]

The whole scene accords with God's having said, ﴾...Then a second blast will be blown, while they are standing and watching* [S 39:68] and *Then there is a single cry, and lo! they are on a plain* [S 79:13-14][75] The *sāhira* is the level earth. After being resurrected they open their eyes and look at the mountains blown away and the seas drained and the earth with no crookedness and no curvature. *Al-amt* [curvature] refers to that which is raised, like a hill, and *al-ᶜawaj* [crookedness] of the earth is a depression, like a lowland. But now the earth becomes level as if it were a sheet of paper, /43/ and the people are amazed when they look at the desert. Each one of them is on his grave, naked and staring in astonishment with his head bowed, pondering and considering the sight. They have no clothes on, as the Messenger of God is recorded in the Ṣaḥīḥ to have said, "People will be resurrected barefooted, naked and uncircumsized, except one group who died as believers away from home and were not shrouded. They are resurrected dressed in clothing from the Garden." So it is with others from the community of Muḥammad who have followed the *sunna* and have not departed from it [by even so much as would pass through] the eye of a needle. For the Messenger of God said, "Take great care in clothing your dead, for my community will be raised in their shrouds, while the rest of the nations are naked." Abū Sufyān[76] related that on good authority. And the Prophet also said, "The dead person will be raised in his clothes." This latter seems to us to be the most credible of what has been reported.

One person, knowing he was about to die, said, "Dress me in such and such clothing." His wishes were not carried out, however, so that he died in a nightshirt with nothing /44/ else on. After a few days he was seen in a dream, appearing to be very sad. "How are you?" he was asked, but he refused to say much, replying only, "You have denied me my clothing, therefore you cause me to be raised up in this nightshirt and nothing else!"[77]

CHAPTER [This section concerns] the period between the two soundings of the trumpet. Here is the second death, because it involves constraint of the inner senses, while the bodily death is constraint of the outer senses. For although the bodies perform physical movements, they do not themselves actually pray or fast or worship. Even if an angel were made to enter a corpse it would not stay there because of its desire to take form in its own world. The soul is a simple substance, and when it is linked to the body, life and activity automatically follow.

There are differences of opinion concerning the length of time between the two blasts of the trumpet. /45/ The majority agree that it is forty years, but one whose knowledge and wisdom cannot be doubted told me that no one finally knows the duration of that period but God, as it is one of the divine secrets. He also told me that the sole exception to this is reserved by God for Himself. I asked him the meaning of the Prophet's having said, "I will be the first for whom the earth will be cleft on the day of resurrection, and I find my brother Moses taking hold of the foot of the Throne. I do not know if he will be resurrected ahead of me or if he is among those whom God exempts." He replied, "This saying is not an exception to what we have already affirmed about the resurrection of the souls without bodies, because Moses at that time will not have a body." Perhaps the exemption with which the Prophet was concerned relates to the question of dread.[78] For humanity at the time of the lightening-bolt will be terrified, as Kaʿb once said concerning that situation when he was in the council of ʿUmar ibn al-Khaṭṭāb,[79] "O Ibn al-Khaṭṭāb, even if you could claim the works of seventy prophets, I think that you would not be saved from that day." For no one will be saved from the day /46/ except the people whom God exempts from the enormity of the terror and the lightening bolt. They are the people of the fourth station, and there is no doubt that Moses is one of them.

The exemption is from the experience of fear, not from being alive. For if there were at that time anyone who could respond to God when he was asked, "To Whom belongs the kingdom this day?" he would cry, "To You Who are One alone, victorious!"

CHAPTER At that moment everyone is equal, each sitting upon his grave. Among them are the naked and the clothed, the black and the white. There are some whose light is like a weak lamp, some whose light is like a strong shining lamp, some whose light is like a bright star, some whose light is like the moon, and some whose light is like the light of the sun.[80] Each one of them remains with his head bowed, unaware of what is happening to him; this continues for a thousand years until there appears from the West a light accompanied by a tremendous noise. And the heads of all creatures -- humans, *jinn*, birds and beasts -- turn in astonishment toward it. /47/

Then the works of each creature come and say to him, "Rise up and prepare for the resurrection!"[81] At that time whoever has [done] good deeds will see them like a ship on which he can ride. But there are some whose deeds appear in the form of a mule, or a donkey, or a ram on which one sometimes can ride but from which he sometimes gets thrown.

Each of them is given a radiating light in front of him, as well as another like it on his right, shining ahead into the shadows. This conforms to His word, ‹... their light goes forward in front of them and on their right...› [S 66:8]. There is no light on their left, only black shadows, impenetrable by human eyesight. The *kāfir*s are lost in it and the doubters try to draw away from it, but the believer sees into the intensity of its blackness and the depth /48/ of its darkness, praising God for the light he has been given to guide him through that difficulty and to remain before him. For God reveals to the blessed and faithful servant the conditions of those wretched ones who are punished, in order to make absolutely clear to him the superior way. Thus it was written about the people of the Garden and the people of the Fire, ❮Then he looked and saw him in the midst of Hell.❯ [S 37:55] He also has said, ❮Then their eyes turned toward the companions of the Fire, saying, "Our Lord! do not place us among the evildoers!"❯ [S 7:47] There are four things whose value is known only to four [categories of people]: none knows the value of life except the dead, none knows the value of health except the sick, none knows the value of youth except the aged, and none knows the value of abundance except the poor.[82]

There are also some people whose lights go along on their feet and on the tips of their fingers; sometimes they are extinguished, and other times they burn brightly. The lights of individuals at the resurrection are in direct proportion to their faith, and the speed of their steps in proportion to their good works.

The Messenger of God was asked, "How are people resurrected, O Messenger /49/ of God?" He replied, "Two on a camel and three on a camel and four on a camel and five on a camel and ten on a camel." The meaning of that *ḥadīth*, which God knows best, is that God has mercy on those who are in Islam and creates for them out of their works a camel on which they ride. This reference is actually to the works considered weak, since they have to ride several together on a camel. They are like people going out on a far journey; no one of them having the wherewithal to buy an animal, they ride all together along the road. But how can the camel, with ten men on it, reach the destination? This is what is meant by weak deeds, as for example when one holds tightly to his money refusing to give it in alms. But even with that, God ordains him to safety [if he is in the community of Islam]

So do the work to which God has guided you, that there may be a special camel for you alone, and know that such is a profitable enterprise!

The pious travelers are in accord with the word of al-Jalīl, ⁅On that day We shall see gathered those who are righteous /50/ before the All-Merciful in a delegation.⁆ [S 19:85] A rare narrative[83] relates that the Messenger of God said to his companions, "There was once a Jew who did so many good works that he will be resurrected among all of you." The companions replied, "O Messenger of God, what did he do?" He answered, "He inherited a great deal of money from his father, and he spent it on a garden which he devoted entirely to the poor, saying, 'This is my garden in the presence of God.' Then he distributed many gold pieces among those in bad circumstances, saying, 'With this I purchase a slavegirl with God, be He exalted, and male slaves! Then he set free many captives, saying, 'These are my servants with God.' One day he noticed a person who was blind, and saw him sometimes walking and sometimes falling flat. So he bought a riding animal for the man to travel on, saying, 'This is my animal for me to ride in the presence of God.' By Him in Whose hand is my life, I can almost see it coming with saddle and bridle so that he can ride it and travel toward the place of resurrection!"

It is said /51/ in the explanation of His word, ⁅Is the one who walks with his head bowed better guided, or the one who walks evenly on the straight path?⁆ [S 67:22] that it is a parable which God has drawn to the day of resurrection concerning the gathering together of the *mu'min*s and the *kāfir*s. And His having said, ⁅We shall drive the sinners into *jahannam* like a thirsty herd⁆ [S 19:86] is said to mean walking on their faces, because the One Who makes them walk in this world on their feet has the power to make them walk in the hereafter on their faces. This is the interpretation of some of the Qur'ān commentators, and it is supported by His word, ﴾...We shall gather them together on the day of resurrection on their faces...﴿ [S 17:97] But the matter is not as they have said; the real meaning is that the sinner sometimes walks and sometimes topples over on his face. That is explained further in that God mentioned feet when He said, ﴾...and their feet [will bear witness against them] for what they have done.﴿ [S 24:24]

For the phrase ﴾...blind, dumb and deaf...﴿ [S 17:97][84] there is an interpretation different from that favored by the commentators, one that departs from the symbolic expression to which we have called your attention. You may have noticed that the Arabs use this expression, saying, "So and so walks on his face", meaning that he has fallen forward. The actual meaning of "blind" here is that one is removed from the light that shines /52/ in front of believers, and does not share their faith. The intent cannot be total blindness, because there is no question about their seeing the sky rent asunder with the clouds and the angels descending and the mountains levelled and the stars spread out and all of the conditions of the day of resurrection. This is the interpretation of His saying, ﴾Is this sorcery, or do you not see?﴿ [S 52:15], and it means that the blind at the resurrection are those who are plunged into darkness and prevented from gazing at the Generous One,[85] even though the light of God radiates the white earth. A covering is placed upon their eyes so that they can see nothing of that [amazing sight].

And in the same way their ears are covered so that they cannot hear the word of God and the angels crying, ﴾...you will have no fear or sadness on that day...enter the Garden, you and your spouses, rejoicing!﴿ [S 43:68, 70]

They are also deprived of speech as if they were dumb, such as is explained by His saying, ⟨That day they will not be able to speak, nor will they be allowed to offer excuses.⟩ [S 77:35-6] They will be completely helpless, weak and unable to do a thing. Even if they actually had the capability, it would be as if it were lacking, a condition without a condition, [as it were].

There are some people who are raised up with their earthly /53/ temptations. One person may be tempted by the *ᶜūd*,[86] to which he was devoted in his life. When such a one is resurrected from his grave he will take the *ᶜūd* in his right hand and fling it from him, saying, "Away with you! you have kept me from the remembrance of God!" But it will return to him and say, "I am your companion ⟨...until God decides between us, and He is the best of judges.⟩ [S 7:87; cf.10:109] In the same way the drunkard will be raised drunk, and the piper piping. Every one again finds himself in the condition which turned him away from the path of God. Similar to this is the *ḥadīth* related in the Ṣaḥīḥ which says that the drinker of wine will be raised up with the wine-pot hanging from his neck, cup in hand, while he will smell fouler than any corpse on the face of the earth, and every creature who passes by him will curse him.

The dead are also raised with the evidence of any injustices done to them; the Ṣaḥīḥ relates that the one killed in the service of God will arrive on the day of resurrection with his wounds flowing -- the blood with the color of blood but the smell /54/ of musk -- until he finally comes before God.

Then the angels hand over the dead in groups and bands, each individual raised in his own state, mounted on that which has been ordained for him.[87] They are gathered without distinction, the first [to die mixed in] with the last. The Glorious One orders the angels of the near heaven to take care of them. Every one of them takes one of the resurrected, including people, *jinn*, animals and birds. They transport them to the second earth, which is an earth white with silvery light. The angels rank behind the creatures in one great ring, and they number more than ten times the people of the earth. Then God gives a command to the angels of the second earth, and they make a single circle around them all. They number twenty times the others. Then the angels of the third heaven descend and surround /55/ them all in a single circle, and they are thirty times the others in number. Then the angels of the fourth heaven descend and circle behind them all, making a single ring and numbering forty times more than the others. They are followed by the angels of the fifth, sixth and seventh heavens who all descend and circle behind them in single circles, numbering fifty, sixty and seventy times respectively more than all the rest.

At that time all of creation blends and mixes together, one on top of the other, until one foot is raise above a thousand other feet by the density of the throng And people are plunged into sweat of different kinds, up to their chins or their chests or their groins or their shoulders or their knees.[88] Some are overcome by a ligh perspiration, as if seated in a hot bath, and others by moisture as happens to the thirsty person when he drinks water. Those who are wet with sweat are those who have thrones [*manābir*],[89] those with light perspiration are those who have chairs, those [up to their] /56/ ankles are those who died of drowning. The angels call to them, saying ﴾...you will have no fear on that day, neither wil you be sad.﴿ [S 43:68] Someone knowledgeable about such things told me that they are the repentant, like Fuḍayl ibn ʿIyāḍ[90] and others. The Prophet used to say that the one who repents of sins is as if he had no sin, and that is the generally accepted opinion. These, then, are the three kinds -- the people with a great amount of sweat, those with light perspiration and those in sweat up to their ankles. They have white faces, while the faces of the others are black.

How could there not be great agitation, what with the sweat and the sleeplessness, for the sun approaches so close to their heads that one could touch it by extending his hand. The heat of the sun is increased seventy times the normal, as one of the ancestors said, "If the sun rose over the earth the way it will on the day of resurrection, the earth would be charred and the rocks would melt and the rivers would dry up."

So all of creation is in a great commotion, on that white /57/ earth which God mentioned when He said, ❴The day when the earth will be changed into something not the earth...❵ [S 14:48]. People are in different groups at the place where they are gathered together. Rulers from among the people of the earth are like atoms, as has been related in a narrative describing the imperious. It is not that they actually become atoms, but that they are stepped on until they resemble atoms in their humiliation and debasement.

Some people are drinking water which is cold, sweet and clear; this is because children move around their parents with cups of water from the rivers of the Garden for them to drink.[91] One of the ancestors has related that while he was sleeping he dreamed of the coming of the resurrection. It was as if he were actually there, parched of thirst, and he saw small boys giving drink to people. "I called to them," he related, "saying 'Give me a drink of water.' And one of them said to me, 'Do you have a son among us?' 'No,' I answered. 'Then No!' came the reply." Therein /58/ is the advantage of marriage.[92] We have mentioned these children who give drink to the thirsty people in the Kitāb al-Iḥyā'.

A shadow is spread over the heads of certain people keeping the heat away from them. These are the good and sincere folk. For them this condition continues for a thousand years, until they hear the sound of the horn [*nāqūr*], which we have described in the Kitāb al-Iḥyā', and which is one of the mysteries of the Qur'ān.[93] At this sound hearts are terrified and eyes are filled with fear, so strong is its blast. The heads of believers and *kāfir*s alike turn expectantly toward it, thinking that this is a punishment intended to augment the terror of the day of resurrection.

Then eight angels come bearing the Throne, the measure of their pace being equal to the distance traveled in 20,000 years. The various groups of angels and cloud give glory to God with voices so filled with great excitement that one cannot imagine it, until the Throne is settled on that white earth which God created for this special purpose. Then heads /59/ bow, souls are silent and all creation is afraid -- even the prophets are terrified and the *ᶜulamā'* are filled with fear and the saints and martyrs seek to flee from the punishment of God against which nothing can prevail.

And while they are like that, they are flooded by a light from God greater than the light of the sun to whose heat they were subjected. They continue to be very restless and agitated, all together, for a thousand years, with the Glorious One, glorified be He, speaking not a single word to them. So the people go to Adam and say to him, "O Adam, O father of mankind, this matter is lasting a long time!" (As for the *kāfir*, he says, "O my Lord, release me, even if it be to the Fire, from the intensity of the terror seen!") Then they say, "O Adam, you are the one whom God created by His hand, /60/ and to whom He caused His angels to bow down, breathing His spirit into you. Seek forgiveness for us with your Lord in the meting out of judgment, for the situation has gone on and on, and the press of the throng has intensified. Let all come to pass as God wills and let His desires be fulfilled." So Adam says to them, "Truly I disobeyed God when He forbade me to eat of the Tree,[94] therefore I am ashamed to speak to Him about this matter. But go to Noah [Nūḥ], for he is the first of the messengers."[95] So they stop for a thousand years, taking counsel with each other concerning what is going on. Then they go to Noah and say to him, "You are the first of the messengers," mentioning to him the same things they told Adam and seeking his intercession in adjudicating between them. Noah answers them, "Truly I cried out unto God, by which I caused all the people of the earth to be drowned. So I am ashamed before God /61/ to ask Him such a thing.[96] But hurry along to Abraham, for he is the friend of the Merciful One [*khalīl al-Raḥmān*], and ✱...he is the one who gave you the name of Muslims from before...✱ [S 22:78]; perhaps he will intercede for you."

So they take counsel with each other for a thousand years, then go to Abraham, saying to him, "O Abraham, O father of the Muslims, you are the one whom God has taken as His beloved [*khalīl*], so intercede for us with Him. Perhaps He will render judgment with respect to creation." And Abraham replied to them, "I lied three times in the matter of Islam;[97] I disputed with [my people] about the *dīn* of God, and I am embarrassed before God to ask intercession in this situation. But go to Moses, for God took him as spokesman [*kalīm*] and drew him near as confidant. It may be that he will intercede for you."

So again they take counsel with each other for a thousand years while the intensity of their circumstance increases and the place becomes more confined. Then they go to Moses and say to him, "O Son of ᶜImrān, you are the one whom God took as spokesman. He drew you near as confidant and revealed to you the Torah; so intercede for us with your Lord in the meting out of judgment, for the situation has gone on and on and the press of the crowd has intensified; we are being stepped on and the people of *kufr* and *islām* alike are crying out in the depths of longing." But Moses answers them, /62/ saying, "Truly I asked God to punish the people of Pharaoh by years[98] and to make them an example to others, and I also killed someone.[99] Therefore I am ashamed before God to ask intercession with Him in this matter, because of the secret conversation that has passed between us. In this conversation there appeared a suggestion of damnation [*halak*], except that He is the possessor of bounteous mercy and is the Lord of forgiveness. But go to Jesus, for of all the messengers he gives the greatest certainty and is the most knowledgeable about God, the purest in asceticism, and the most profound in wisdom. Perhaps he will intercede for you."

So they take counsel with each other for a thousand years while the intensity of the circumstance increases and the place becomes even more straitened, saying, "How long must we go from messenger to messenger and from one noble being to another?" Then they go to Jesus and say to him, "You are the Spirit of God and His Word and you are the one whom He has designated as leader of this world and the next. So intercede for us in the meting out of judgment." But Jesus says, "Truly my mother and I have been taken as gods, apart from God.[100] How could I intercede for you when I have been worshipped along with Him and designated as His son and He called my father? Do you not see that if one of you has a purse containing some money and there is a seal on it, he is unable to get /63/ to what is in the purse before the seal is broken?" They reply, "Yes, O prophet of God." So he says to them, "Go to the chief of the messengers, the seal of the prophets[101] the brother of the Arabs. For his prayer is reserved as an intercession for his community; his own people caused him great suffering by bruising his forehead, breaking his teeth[102] and setting up a relationship between him and the *jinn*.[103] But he is the highest of them all in glory and the greatest of them in nobility. He used to say, as al-Ṣiddīq[104] said to his brothers, ‡No reproach is upon you this day, for God forgives you and He is the most merciful of those who have mercy.‡ [S 12:92]" Then Jesus begins to recite for them the virtues of the Prophet. Because their ears are willing to hear, their souls are filled with desire to go to him.

So they come to his throne and they say to him, "O Messenger of God, you are the beloved of God and the beloved is the most excellent of mediators, so intercede for us with God.[105] For we went to our father Adam and he sent us to Noah; we went to Noah and he sent us to Abraham; we went to Abraham and he sent us to Moses; we went to Moses and he sent us to Jesus. So we went to Jesus and he sent us to you, may the blessing and peace of God be upon you. After you there is no one else to ask and apart from you no place of refuge."

And the Prophet says, "I am the right one! I am the right one [to intercede] insofar as God allows it for whomever He wills and chooses." Proceeding /64/ toward the pavilions of God, the Prophet asks permission and it is granted to him. Then the veils are raised and he enters into the Throne, falling down in prostration; and the prostration lasts for a thousand years, while he is praising God with praise such as no one has ever before offered. One of the gnostics said that that is the praise with which God praised Himself on the day in which He concluded His creation; the Throne trembles in tribute to Him. This has been treated previously in the Iḥyā'.

Meanwhile the place where the people are waiting becomes increasingly confined, and as their situation gets worse their fear intensifies and terror comes over them in waves. The things about which they had been niggardly on earth now surround each one of them. The one who refused to give a camel as alms carries on his back a braying camel weighing as much as a huge mountain The one who refused the almsgiving of a cow carries on his back a bellowing bull as heavy as a huge mountain. The one who refused to give a sheep carries on his back a bleating ewe, the weight of a huge mountain. The one who refused to give a goat bears on his back a bleating and crying billygoat again as heavy as a huge mountain. The braying and the bellowing and the bleating and the crying are like roaring thunder.

The one who refused to offer crops in alms carries on his back a pair of sacks filled /65/ with the things he used to withhold, either wheat or barley, crying out from under it in affliction and lament. And the one who refused the almsgiving of money carries a bald monster with *zabībatān*,[106] its tail falling into his nose and coiling around his neck; it is so heavy on his shoulders that he might have put on a necklace of all the mill-stones on earth. Everyone is crying out,"What is this?" and the angels reply to them, "This is what you held on to so tightly while on the earth, being greedy and niggardly about it!" Thus has He said, ❴...That which they held on to will be tied to their necks on the day of resurrection...❵ [S 3:180]

There are some for whom the pudenda enlarge and pus streams out, their neighbors becoming nauseated from the putrid smell. Others are impaled on stakes of fire, while the tongues of still others hang out on their chests in a repulsive fashion. These are the fornicators the sodomites and the liars. The bellies of some people swell like huge mountains; they are the usurers. To whomever has sinned, /66/ the likeness of his sin appears in visible form.

CHAPTER Then the Glorious One, glorified be He, calls: "O Muḥammad, lift your head and speak, for you will be heard; seek intercession and it will be granted." So the Prophet says, "O my Lord, adjudicate between your worshippers,[107] for their circumstance has been greatly drawn out and every one of them has been shown his sins in the arena of the resurrection." Then comes the cry, "Yes, O Muḥammad!", and God commands that the Garden be adorned and brought near. So it is brought, with its lovely fresh breezes, the most fragrant and delicious imaginable, that can be felt from a distance of five hundred years.[108] It refreshes the souls and gives life to the hearts, except to those whose works on the earth were evil, for to them its breezes are forbidden. The Garden is placed on the right of the Throne.

Then God commands that the Fire be brought. It shakes with fear and terror and says to the angels sent to it, "Do you know, did God create creation in order that I should suffer by it?" And they say to it, "No, by His power! He has sent us to you so that you might take vengeance on whomever of His creation has disobeyed Him, and for such /67/ a day as this you were created."

So they bring the Fire, which walks on four legs and is bound by seventy thousand reins. On each of the reins are seventy thousand rings; if all the iron in the world were collected it would not equal that of one ring. On every ring are seventy thousand guardians of hell; if even one among them were ordered to level the mountains or to crush the earth he would be able to do it.

The Fire makes sounds like the braying of a donkey, moaning and roaring, with sparks and smoke flaring up so that the horizons are covered by darkness. And when there is still the distance of a thousand years between it and creation, the Fire slips away from the group of the guardians and approaches the people of the place of judgment, clattering and thundering and moaning. "What is that!" one cries. "That is *jahannam*," another replies, "escaped from the hands of the guardians of hell, and so powerful is it that one cannot avoid its grasp!" Everyone falls on his knees, even the messengers. Abraham, Moses and Jesus cling to the Throne, the one forgetting *al-dhabīḥ*,[109] the next forgetting Aaron, and the third forgetting Mary [Maryam]. And each one of them cries, "O Lord, my soul! my soul! I will not ask of you anything else /68/ on this day!"

It is related that even the Messiah says, "O Lord, my soul and my mother! I will not ask of you anything else on this day, for it is the most important thing to me." But the Prophet Muḥammad says, "My community! my community! O Lord, preserve it and save it!"

At the place of judgment there is not a one whose legs can hold him, as He has said, ⁜You will see every community bowing down, for every community is called to its Book of Record...⁜ [S 45:28] At the time when the Fire escapes, everyone falls down [in fear] of its wrath and rage. Thus is his word, ⁜When it sees them from a far distant place, they hear it raging and moaning.⁜ [S 25:12] God has said, ⁜Almost splitting with rage...⁜ [S 67:8], meaning that it is almost cleft in two halves from the intensity of its wrath.

Then by the command of God the Messenger of God appears and seizes the Fire by its halter, saying to it, "Turn around and go back until the crowd comes that is destined for you." And the Fire replies, "Get out of my way, for you, O Muḥammad, are taboo to me!" Then comes a cry from behind the pavilions of al-Jalāl, "Listen to him and obey him!" So the Fire is taken and put on the left side of the Throne. Those gathered at the place of judgment talk about its being taken there and their fear abates some. Thus is /69/ His word, ⁜We have not sent you except as a mercy to the world.⁜ [S 21:107]

So there is a balance set up, and it is made of two scales: a scale on the right of the Throne made of light and a scale on the left of the Throne made of darkness. Then al-Jalīl uncovers His leg.[110] All the people prostrate themselves, glorifying Him out of humility before His greatness, except for the *kāfir*s who were polytheists for the days of their lives, worshipping stones and wood and such things as do not receive the power of God. The vertebrae of their backbones turn to iron so that they are unable to bow down, as He has said, ⁋On the day when the shin is exposed and they are called to fall down in prostration, but are not able to.⁋ [S 68:42] Al-Bukhārī relates in his commentary, citing authority, that the Messenger of God said, "God reveals His leg on the day of resurrection, and all the believers, male and female, bow down."

I have been on guard against all allegorical interpretation of the *ḥadīth* and disclaimed those who reject it.[111] In the same way I have avoided /70/ describing the balance, considering the speech of those who describe it by similies to be in error, and have relegated it to the concerns of the Malakūtī world. For good and evil actions are accidents[112] and the weight of accidents cannot be gauged for certain but by a Malakūtī balance.

While people are bowing down in prostration, the Glorious One calls in a voice that can be heard by those far off as well as those who are near: "I am the King! I am the Judge!" Al-Bukhārī related that God says, "The injustice of an oppressor does not surpass Me, for if it surpassed Me, I would be the oppressor."

Then He judges the beasts and takes vengeance on the horned on behalf of the hornless. Separating the wild animals and the birds, He says to them, "Become as dust" as He spreads them level on the earth.[113] At that time ⁋...those who rejected and disobeyed the Messenger will wish that they could be made level with the earth...⁋ [S 4:42] and the *kāfir* will long for it, saying, ⁋...Oh, if only I could be dust!"⁋ [S 78:40]

Then the cry goes out from in front of God, "Where is the preserved tablet [*lawḥ al-maḥfūẓ*]?" It is brought to Him, and it is greatly agitated. So God says, "Where is that which has been recorded upon you from the Torah [*tawrāt*], and the Psalms [*zabūr*], /71/ and the Gospel [*injīl*], and the Qur'ān [*furqān*]?" And the tablet replies, "The trusted spirit [Gabriel] took it from me." So Gabriel is brought, his legs and shoulders trembling and shaking, and God says, "O Gabriel, this tablet claims that you carried away from it My word and My revelation. Is it telling the truth?" Gabriel answers, "Yes, O Lord." So God says, "And what have you done with it?" to which Gabriel replies, "I gave the Torah to Moses and the Psalms to David [Dā'ūd] and the Gospel to Jesus and the Qur'ān to Muḥammad. And I gave to each messenger his message; to those who have received a revelation I gave that which has been revealed."

Then comes the cry, "O Noah!" and he is brought, his legs and shoulders trembling and shaking. God says, "O Noah, Gabriel claims that you are one of the messengers." "He is correct," says Noah, and then he is asked, "What have you done with regard to your people?" He answers, "❨...I have called to them night and day, but my call only increases their flight.❩ [S 71:5-6]" Then the cry comes, "O people of Noah!" They are brought in a group and told, "This your brother Noah claims that he imparted the message to you." They reply, "O our Lord, he is lying. Nothing was communicated to us!" and they deny the message. So God says, "O Noah, do you have any evidence against them?" "Yes, O Lord," he answers, "my proof against them is Muḥammad and his community." "How is that?" they all ask. "We are the first of the communities and they are the last." Then the Prophet Muḥammad is brought and God says to him, "O Muḥammad, this is Noah /72/ who calls upon you to testify. Will you witness to his having transmitted the message?" So the Prophet recites, ❨Truly I have sent Noah to his people...❩ [S 71:1], to the end of the *sūra*. Then al-Jalīl says [to the people of Noah], "Truth must be enjoined on you, and the word of punishment must be levied against the *kāfir*s."

So He orders them all as a group to the Fire, without weighing individual deeds and without passing individual judgment.

Then He calls, "Where is cĀd?"[114] And his people do with Hūd as the people of Noah did with Noah. So the Prophet testifies against them, along with the best of his community, reciting, ⟨cĀd gave the lie to the messengers⟩ [S 26:123], until the end of the story. Then God orders them as a single group to the Fire.

Then He calls, "O Ṣāliḥ, and O Thamūd!" They are brought and he testifies against them concerning those things that they denied. So the Prophet recites, ⟨Thamūd gave the lie to the messengers⟩ [S 26:141], to the end of the story. And God does to them the same as to the others. /73/ One community after another comes out -- the Qur'ān has told about them by way of illustration, and mentioned them as a reminder, as He has said, ⟨...and many generations between them⟩ [S 25:38] and ⟨Then We sent our messengers in succession; every time a community's messenger came, they gave him the lie...⟩ [S 23:44] and ⟨...and those after them; only God knows. To them came their messengers with clear signs...⟩ [S 14:9] In this there is a warning for those oppressive eras as [those of] the people of --------[115] and those like them, until the call reached the people of Rass and Tubbac[116] and the people of Abraham. In each case they are not weighed on the balance nor is the reckoning applied to them; ⟨...on that day will they be veiled from their Lord⟩ [S 83:15] This is the interpretation given, because God cannot punish those whom He has seen or to whom He has spoken.

Then He calls to Moses ibn cImrān and he is brought to Him, trembling as if he were /74/ a piece of paper in a blowing wind, with his face yellowed and his knees shaking. And He says to him, "O Ibn cImrān, Gabriel claims that he communicated to you the message and the Torah. Can you witness to this communication?" "Yes!"

is the reply. God says, "Return to your throne and recite what has been revealed to you from the Book of your Lord." So he goes back to the throne and recites, while all who are in the place of resurrection listen to him. The Torah comes forth from him fresh and new with the same excellence as on the day it was revealed, so it seems to the rabbis [*al-aḥbār*] as if they had never before heard it.

Then God calls, "O David!" And he comes, fearful as if he were a piece of paper trembling in a blowing wind, with shaking knees and yellowed face. And God says "O David, Gabriel claims that he communicated to you the Psalms. Can you witness to this communication?" "Yes, O Lord," he replies. Then God says to him, "Go to your throne and recite what has been revealed to you." So he goes and recites, and his voice is the most beautiful of all men. In the Ṣaḥīḥ it says that he is the master psalmist among the people of the Garden.

Then the one killed before the Ark /75/ of God's presence[117] hears his voice, bursts through the crowd and crosses over the rows of people until he reaches David. He hangs on to him, saying, "Did the Psalms not admonish you, that you still intended ill for me?" David becomes very embarrassed and is silent, dumbfounded. And the place of resurrection trembles because of what the people see happening to David. Then Uriah [Ūriyā'] takes hold of David and urges him on to God. The veil is drawn aside for them, and Uriah says, "O Lord, render justice to me from him.[118] For he singled me out for destruction and made me fight before al-Tābūt so that I was killed, then he married my wife, even though at the time he had ninety-nine others." So God turns to David and says to him, "Is he telling the truth?" And David answers, "Yes, O Lord. It was thus." And his head is lowered in shame before God and in expectation of the punishment to come from Him. Yet he is also hopeful because of God's promis of forgiveness. When he is afraid his head is lowered in shame before God, but when hope fills him he raises his head. Then God says to his companion, "I have given you in compensation such and such palaces, and such and such of the *ḥūr* and the beautiful youths;[119] /76/ are you satisfied?" He answers, "Yes, O Lord, I am satisfied." Then He says to David, "Go, for I have forgiven you." Thus does God do with those whom He has honored. From the extent of His sustenance, He accords to them the greatest of His pardon. God then says to David, "Return to your throne and recite the remainder of the Psalms." So he goes then and carries out God's order. God commands of the tribe of Israel that they be divided into two groups -- one the group of believers and the one the group of evildoers.

Then He cries out, "Where is Jesus, son of Mary?" Jesus is brought, and He says to him, ﴾...Did you say to people, 'Take me and my mother as gods, apart from God' ...?﴿[S 5:116]" Jesus lauds God as God would wish and extols Him with great praise. Then he rebukes and reviles himself, and says, "﴾...Glory be to you! It is not for me to say what I have no right to say. Had I said it, You would have known it. You know what is in my soul, though I do not know what is in Yours. Truly You are the One Who knows the unseen.﴿ [S 5:116]" Then God smiles and says, "﴾...On this day those who are truthful will profit from their truthfulness...﴿ [S 5:119] You are truthful, O Jesus, so go to your throne and recite the Gospel which has been communicated to you by Gabriel." And Jesus responds, "Yes, O Lord." Then he goes back /77/ and recites, and heads are lifted up toward him because of the beauty of his voice and his rendering of it. For he is the most judicious of mankind in relating matters, and he brings the Gospel fresh and new, so that even monks think that they have never known one verse of it. Then the Christians are divided into two groups, the wrongdoers with the wrong-doers and the believers with the believers.

Then the cry goes out, "Where is Muḥammad?" He is brought, and God says to him, "O Muḥammad, Gabriel claims that he has communicated to you the Qur'ān." "Yes, O Lord," is the reply. So God says to him, "Return to your throne and recite." So he recites the Qur'ān and it comes forth from him so fresh and new, with such sweetness and grace, that the believers and the pious rejoice in it. Their faces are ﴾laughing, rejoicing﴿ [S 80:39], while the faces of the wrongdoers are like dust, and rigid.

The proof of this preceding interrogation of the messengers and the communities comes in His saying, ﴾For We shall question those to whom We sent a message, and We shall question the messengers﴿ [S 7:6] and ﴾One day God will gather the messengers and He will say, "What response have you gotten?" They will say, "We have no knowledge; /78/ truly You are the One Who knows the unseen."﴿ [S 5:109] There are two points of view about this: some think that the messengers actually forget the correct response out of fear of what is coming; and some think that they say it in surrender to God, as the Messiah did when he said, ﴾...Had I said it, You would have known it. You know what is in my soul, though I do not know what is in Yours. Truly you are the One Who knows the unseen.﴿ [S 5:116] The first is the best explanation, as we have related in <u>al-Iḥyā'</u>, because the messengers contend with each other for superiority; and the Messiah is among the most illustrious of them because he is the word of God and His spirit.

When the Prophet recites the Qur'ān, it seems to the [members of the] community that they have never before heard it. Someone once said to Aṣmaʿī,[120] "You assert that you have memorized the Book of God better than anyone," to which he replied, "O son of my brother, on the day I hear it from the Messenger of God, it will be as if I had never heard it at all."

When the reading of the Book is concluded, the cry comes from behind the pavilions of the Glorious One, "﴾Separate yourselves this day, oh you sinners!﴿ [S 36:50]" The place of resurrection is shaken and a great terror arises there. The angels are mixed up with the *jinn* and the *jinn* with the sons of Adam, and all are in one great clamor.

Then the call goes out, "Adam, /79/ send forth those of your children consigned to the Fire!" "How many, O Lord?" he asks, and God says to him, "Of every thousand, nine hundred and ninety-nine go to the Fire and one to the Garden." So he continues to pull out from the rest the heretics and the negligent and the corrupt, until there remains only a handful of the Lord, as al-Ṣadīq [Abū Bakr] said, "We are a handful of the Lord." Then the others are bound together with the demons.

For some people the balance is set up, and there the bad deeds of each outweigh the good deeds. Everyone to whom the Law came is inevitably brought to the balance. And when they are segregated and are certain that they are doomed, they say, "Adam has wronged us and the myrmidons have seized us by the forelock."[121] Then comes the cry from before God, "﴾...There is no injustice on this day. Truly God is swift in reckoning.﴿ [S 40:17]" A huge Book is pulled out for them, filling up the entire space between East and West, in which are recorded all of the acts of the creatures. There is no thing ﴾...small or large but what is accounted for. They will find [a record of] what they did, ready for them; and your Lord will treat no one unjustly.﴿ [S 18:49] That means that the deeds of creation are shown each day to God. Then God orders his noble and pure angels to transcribe them into the great Book, as /80/ He has said, ﴾...Truly We have transcribed all that you do.﴿ [S 45:29]

Then He calls to them individual by individual, and takes account of every one of them. Their feet and hands bear testimony, as He said ﴾This day shall their tongues and their hands and their feet bear witness to what they have done.﴿ [S 24:24]

It says in the tradition that one person among them stops in front of God, Who says to him, "O you servant of evil, you are a disobedient wrongdoer!" He asks, "What have I done?" and God says, "There is evidence against you." Then his recorders are brought. "They lie about me!" he protests, and he argues his cause, as God has said, ﴾On the day when each soul is brought he will dispute concerning himself...﴿ [S 16:111] And then his mouth will be sealed, as He has said, ﴾On that day We shall put a seal on their mouths, and their hands will speak to us and their feet will bear witness to what they have acquired.﴿ [S 36:65] So his limbs testify against him and he is ordered to the Fire. Then his limbs begin to rebuke him, saying, "It is not our choice, ﴾...God has made us speak; it is He Who makes everything speak ...﴿ [S 41:21]"

After this is concluded, they are pushed into the vaults of *jahannam*, and their voices break out in weeping and uproar. A great clamor is roused in them when the monotheists and the believers appear to them surrounded by angels, every one of them reciting and saying to them, ﴾...This is your day which /81/ you have been promised.﴿ [S 21:103] The greatest terror comes at four particular instances: at the blowing of the trumpet, at the escape of Hell from the hands of its keepers, at the bringing forth of the resurrection of Adam, and at the driving away of those [mentioned above] into the vaults [of *jahannam*].

Then only the believers, the Muslims, the doers of good works, the gnostics, the affirmers of revelation [*ṣiddīqūn*], the martyrs, the righteous and the messengers remain at the place of resurrection. There are no doubters among them, nor hypocrites, nor Zindīqs.[122] Then God says, "O people of the place of resurrection, Who is your Lord?" They answer, "God!" and He says to them, "Do you know Him?" They reply, "Yes!" Then an angel is revealed to them at the left of the Throne, so large that one could put the seven seas into the hollow of his thumb and they would not be visible. And he says to them, by God's command, "I am your Lord!" But they answer, "We take refuge in God from you!" Then an angel appears to them at the right of the Throne, so large that one could put the fourteen seas into the hollow of his thumb and they would not be visible. And he says, by God's order, "I am your Lord!" But they reply, "We take refuge in God from you!"

Then the Lord Himself appears to them in a form other than that in which they know Him and He says to them, "I am your Lord!" But they seek refuge in God from Him. Finally He appears to them in the form in which they have known and heard about Him. He smiles and they all bow down in prostration before Him, /82/ and He says, "Welcome to you." Then He moves along with them to the Garden, and they follow Him and He passes over the Ṣirāṭ with them.[123] The people are in troups: the messengers, then the prophets, then the affirmers of revelation, then the doers of righteousness, then the martyrs, then the believers, then the gnostics. There will remain those Muslims among them who are prostrate on their faces, those who are confined on the Aᶜrāf[124], and some of them are folk who fell short of the completeness of faith. Some of these will cross the bridge of Ṣirāṭ in a hundred years, and others will cross it in a thousand, yet despite all that, the Fire will not burn any one who has seen his Lord with his eyes; his vision keeps him from harm.

We have already talked about the circumstance of each of the Muslims and believers and the beneficent in our book entitled al-Istidrāj.[125] They are in an unrestrained crowd, moving back and forth with recurring hunger and thirst. Their lives disintegrate and their breath is like smoke. They drink from the Basin [*ḥawḍ*][126] out of cups as numerous as the stars in the sky, the water coming /83/ from the river of Kawthar.[127] The extent of it is the same as from Jerusalem to Ṣanᶜā', from Aden to Medina. Thus the Prophet said, "My throne is at the Basin, i.e. on one edge of it, in terms of measurement and weight and extent. Those who are driven away from it are preoccupied at the bridge of Ṣirāṭ by the evil of their shameful deeds."

How many a person performing ablutions does not complete them well, and does not ask about the purity of the water used! And how many a one who prays does not genuinely inquire into his prayers, rather performing them by rote with no feeling of submission or humility! If an ant bites him he turns around. But as for those who know the majesty of God -- should their hands and feet be cut off they would not move, such is their preoccupation with reverence and contemplation. They know the rank of Him before whom they stand.

It might happen that a man is stung by a scorpion in the courtroom of a prince, but he does not dare move and he is patient /84/ and respectful to the prince in that room. Such is the human situation with respect to a creature like him who has no power to harm or to aid his soul. So what, then, is the situation of the one who stands before God and His majesty and power and greatness and might! A story is told concerning the secretary of one of the sultans. When a prince threw something at him and the point of it pierced his foot, he was undisturbed and did not move until the prince got up. Yet, had an ant bitten him during his prayer, he would have turned around and rubbed it off! Such is the disdain for what is due the majesty of God, be He exalted. Therefore the one who is heedless in this fashion is not allowed to pass over the bridge of Ṣirāṭ. (In these narratives it is not necessary to describe completely the neglect of the performances of religious duty.)

There is also a story about a transgressor who knows that he is to come before God. His acts of injustice are brought to him, and those things in which he was ill-treated attach themselves to him. So God says to him, "Look above your head, O you to whom injustice has been done, /85/ for there is a palace so great that it astounds the vision." He says to him, "What is this, O Lord?" and God replies, "It is for sale. Buy it from Me." "I do not have the price with me," says the man, so God replies, "If you desist from oppressive acts toward your brother, the palace will be yours." And the man says, "I have done it, O Lord." Thus does God deal with repentant sinners, as is His word, ❴...Truly He forgives those who repent.❵ [S 17:25] The repenter is the one who refrains from erring and never returns to it. David has been called a repenter, as have others of the messengers[128] in the narrative about the people of the place of resurrection. Mention has already been made of the different interpretations concerning this.

In the Ṣaḥīḥ it says that the first thing God decides concerns cases of bloodshed, and the first to be given their recompense, are those who have lost their vision. On the day of resurrection God calls to the blind and says to them, "You are the most appropriate, that is, the most worthy to look at Us." Then He gives them life and says to them, "Go to My right." A white banner is awarded to them and put in the hand of Shu^{c}ayb,[129] who goes /86/ in front of them. With them are angels of light, whose number only God can calculate, conducting them in solemn procession as one would lead a bride; they pass on with them to the Ṣirāṭ with the speed of lightening. Each of them is characterized by patience, forbearance and knowledge, as were Ibn ʿAbbās[130] and those like him in this community.[131]

Then the call comes, "Where are the people of affliction? He wants those who have infirmities!" So they are brought and God revivifies them with a salutation in the sweetest of tongues; then He orders them to His right. To them is given a green banner, put in the hand of Job [Ayyūb], and he goes before them on the right. Those who have suffered are characterized by patience, forbearance and knowledge, as were ʿAqīl ibn Abī Ṭālib,[132] and those like him in this community.

Then comes the call, "Where are the people of righteousness?" They are brought to God and He welcomes them, saying what He wishes to say. Then He orders them to His right; a red banner is given to them, put in the hand of Joseph, who goes in front of them on the right. The righteous are characterized by patience, forbearance and knowledge, as were Rāshid ibn Sulaymān and those like him in this community.

Then comes the call, "Where are those who love God?" They are brought to God and He welcomes them, saying what He wishes to say. Then He orders them to His right; a yellow banner is given them, placed in the hand of Aaron, and he goes before them on the right. Those who love God are characterized by /87/ patience and knowledge and forbearance, never annoyed nor displeased with any earthly circumstances, as were Abū Turāb (by whom I mean ʿAlī ibn Abī Ṭālib)[133] and those like him in this community.

Then the call comes, "Where are those who weep out of fear of God?" They are brought to God, and their tears when weighed against the blood of the martyrs and the ink of the *ʿulamāʾ* tip the balance. So He orders them to His right; a multi-colored banner is given them, because they wept for different reasons -- one cried out of fear, another out of desire and a third in remorse. The banner is put in the hand of Noah. The *ᶜulamā'* are distressed at this priority over them and they say, "It is our knowledge that has brought about their weeping!" Then comes the cry, "Gently, O Noah!" and the crowd stops.

The ink of the *ᶜulama'* is then balanced against the blood of the martyrs, and the latter outweighs it. So God commands the martyrs to His right, and to them is given a saffron banner, put in the hand of John [Yaḥyá]. Then the *ᶜulamā'* come in front of them, and distressed at this priority over them they say, "It is because of our knowledge that they fought so that in turn they were killed, thus we have more right than they to priority." /88/ So the Glorious One smiles and says to them, "You are with Me as are My prophets. Intercede for whomever you wish." So the *ᶜālim* intercedes for his neighbors and his brethren, and each of them orders an angel to call out among the people, "Here is Fulān, the *ᶜālim*, who has been given permission to intercede for those who have helped him in some way, or who gave him a bite to eat when he was hungry or offered him a drink of water when he was thirsty. Let them stand before him so that he can intercede for them." (For in the Ṣaḥīḥ it says that the first to intercede are the messengers, then the prophets, the the *ᶜulamā'*.) A white banner is given to them, and it is put in the hand of Abraham, for he is the one to whom the most revelations were given.

Then comes the cry, "Where are the poor?" They are brought to God and He says to them, "Greetings to those for whom the world was a prison." Then He orders them to His right and gives them a yellow banner, placed in the hand of Jesus, who goes before them on the right. And still another cry comes, "Where are the rich?" They are brought to God, and He enumerates to them for five hundred years those things that have been given to them;

then He orders them to His right and gives them a multi-colored banner put into the hand of Solomon [Sulaymān], who goes before them on the right. /89/

In the traditions it says that there are four things against which one calls the witness of four [others]. The rich are called, along with those in a state of felicity, and to them is said, "What has kept you from the worship of God?" They reply, "He has given us power and happiness which has kept us from the pursuit of His truth in the earthly domain." Then comes the question, "Who has the greater fortune, you or Solomon?" "Definitely Solomon!" they say, to which the reply is, "But that did not keep him from the pursuit of God's truth and perseverance in remembering Him."

Then comes the question, "Where are the people of tribulation?" They are brought in groups and are asked, "What has prevented you from the worship of God?" They answer, "God has tried us in the earthly domain with all sorts of problems and maladies, keeping us from remembrance of Him and uprightly following His truth." So it is said to them "Who was the more afflicted, you or Job?" They reply, "Job, of course!" And the response comes, "But that did not keep him from following the truth of God and devoting himself to the remembrance of Him."

Then comes the [third] call, "Where are those who are in their prime, the elegant young men and the slaves?" They are brought /90/ and to them is said, "What kept you from the worship of God in the earthly realm?" They gave the reply, "He gave us beauty and lovely things by which we were tempted, and we were thus engaged in other than the pursuit of His truth." Then the slaves speak, saying, "We were occupied in the bonds of slavery on the earth." "Were you the most beautiful, or was Joseph [Yūsuf]?" they are asked. "Naturally Joseph was!" they answer. So the reply comes, "That did not prevent him, though he was in the bonds of slavery, from following God's truth and devoting himself to His memory."

Then comes the [fourth] call, "Where are the poor?" They are brought in groups and the same question is asked, "What kept you from pursuit of God's truth?" They respond by saying, "God tested us in the earthly realm with miserable poverty which kept us from His truth." So they are asked, "Who was the most poor, you or Jesus?" to which they reply, "Jesus was!" And the answer comes, "But that did not keep him /91/ from following God's truth and devoting himself to remembering Him."

So whoever has been tested in one of these four categories, let him remember his companion [the one described here]! The Messenger of God used to say in his prayer, "O God, I take refuge with you from the temptation of riches and poverty." Learn a lesson from the Messiah, for it is said that he had no purse at all, that he was dressed in the same woolen garment for twenty years, and that in his travels he had only a small mug and a comb. One day he saw a man drinking with his hand, so he threw the mug from his hand and never used it again. Then he passed by a man running his fingers through his beard, so he threw away the comb from his hand and never used it after that.[134] He used to say, "My feet are my riding animal, my houses are the caves of the earth, and my food is its plants and my drink its rivers. What riches are greater than this, O sons /92/ of Israel? Eat barley and wild onions, but beware of bread made from wheat, for you will not be grateful for it!"

Thus on the day of resurrection a man is called and God says to him, "What was your condition in the earthly domain?" He replies, "I served You for five hundred years on an island surrounded by the sea. With nothing for company there but the remembrance of You, I fasted and prayed until I died in prostration." So God says to him, "You are telling the truth; enter the Garden by My mercy." But the man answers, "No, O Lord, rather by my acts!" So God says to him, "Come now, so that I may settle the account with you, O servant of mine. Who gave you the ability to worship for five hundred years on an island, fasting and praying?" And he replies, "You, O Lord." Then God says, "Who made a pomegranate tree grow up for you, every day bearing lovely fruits by which you were nourished?" And the man says, "You, O Lord." Then God says, "Who caused springs to gush forth with sweet water on that island surrounded /93/ by the bitter salt sea, such that you could drink of their water and wash from them?" He replied, "You, O Lord." And God continued, "Who answered you when you cried, 'O God, seize my spirit while I pray'?" And he answered, "You, O Lord." Then the balance is raised for him, and the service of five hundred years is not sufficient to outweight the blessing of even one glance, for the brilliance of that glance overbalances it. And God says, "Take him to the Fire." But then He turns him away from that path, and says with a smile, "Enter the Garden by My mercy; you have been a good servant, O My servant."

In the same say a man is brought on the day of resurrection, and his account is settled. Then God orders him to the Fire, but he turns around on the path. So God says to Him, "Come back toward Me!" He comes to Him, and God says, "O evil servant, why did you turn around?" He answers, "O Lord, I used to renounce You, yet I had hope in You; I died, yet I had hope in You; You judged me, yet I had hope in You; You ordered me to the Fire, and still I had hope in You; that is what made me turn toward You." /94/ So God says, "You have hoped generously, and placed your expectation in One Who is generous. Go, for I forgive you."

It may be that forgiveness will come from God at the time of reckoning, and calculation of man's due, except in cases of premeditated killing. That is never forgiven, as *shirk* is not, (unless one enters Islam from *shirk*), except for him who fully repents of the killing and never returns to his wrongful ways. For the killer brings death to the one to whom God has given life.

In some of the revealed books [these words are attributed to God]: "O Son of Adam, how you have done wrong! You have associated with Me in My work. Do you not see what you have done? I give life and you cause death. Wake up, O slayer, for you are competing with Me in a battle!" And in one of the revealed scriptures it says, "O son of Adam, whether you do a deed that is good or evil in My sight, it is I who give you life in death and give you death in life. You desire the feeding of one who is starving, recompense for one who is wronged, /95/ and other such things that arise in the circumstances of life. Killing, then, whether deliberate or accidental, scorns atonement, so beware, for it is a horrendous deed." As for major transgressions[135] intercession may be hoped for those who commit them, once they are rectified and purified.

Those who are more highly esteemed by God are taken out of the Fire after a thousand years, and they are charred black. Al-Ḥasan al-Baṣrī used to say in his discourse, "Oh, that I might be that man!"[136] There is no doubt that he was knowledgeable concerning the judgments of the hereafter.

On the day of resurrection a man is brought whose good deeds do not tip the scale, but are balanced by his evil deeds. So God, out of compassion says to him, "Go among the people and beg for someone to give you a good deed by which I can allow you to enter the Garden." So he goes searching through the worlds, but finds none who will talk to him about it. Everyone he asks says to him, "I fear that my own scale will be lightened [on the credit side]. I have more need of good deeds than you do!" /96/ When he is about to give up hope, someone says to him, "What is it that you are seeking?" He replies, "One good deed. I have passed by people who have thousands of them, but they refused to give me any." So the man says to him, "I have already encountered God, and in my book was found only one good deed. I do not think that it will be any help to me, so take it as a gift from me to you." He hurries away with it, full of joy and delight. Then God says, "How did it go?", though of course He knows. And the man explains that such and such happened to him, "My generosity is broader even than your generosity. Go in the hand of your brother and enter the Garden."

In like manner the two pans of the balance are equal for another man, so God says to him, "You are neither of the people of the Garden nor of the people of the Fire." Just then an angel arrives with a page, placing it on the pan with the evil deeds. On it is written "uff!"[137] Thus the bad deeds outweigh /97/ the good, because that is a word of filial disobedience, outweighing the mountains of the earth. With it he is ordered to the Fire. But the man demands to be taken back to God, so God says, "Return him!" He then asks the man, "O you recalcitrant servant, why do you demand to be returned to Me?" And the man replies, "My God, I saw that I was travelling toward the Fire, with no question about it. Yes, I was disobedient toward my father while on earth. But he is also travelling toward the Fire like me; so double upon me the sins of my father and deliver him from them." Then God smiles and says, "You were disobedient to him on earth, but dutiful toward him in the hereafter. So take your father's hand and enter the Garden."

None go to the Fire without first being stopped by the angels, out of their knowledge of the mysterious laws of the hereafter, so that they may call to people who are despicable and were created to be the firewood and the filling [of the Fire], /98/ "﴾Stop them, for they are to be questioned!﴿" [S 37:24] So that group is held back until the cry goes out to them "﴾What is wrong with you that you do not help one another?﴿" [S 37:25] They give themselves up with tears and confess their transgressions. Thus did He say, ﴾They confess their transgressions, but [mercy is] far removed from the companions of the blaze [*al-saʿīr*].﴿ [S 67:11] When the guardians of hell see them, they are surrendering, all the while moaning and questioning each other, confessing yet complaining loudly of their punishment. Then comes the cry from before God, "﴾...far removed from the companions of the blaze.﴿" [S 67:11] And they are driven in one load to the Fire.

In like manner those from the community of Muḥammad who have committed major transgressions are brought, old men and women, middle-aged men and women and youths. Then Mālik,[138] keeper of the Fire, looks at them and says, "Who are you, assembly of the wretched? What do I see? Your hands are not shackled and you are not wearing fetters or chains, and your faces are not blackened. None has ever come to me in better condition than you!" So they reply, "O Mālik, we are the wretched of the community of Muḥammad. Let us weep over our sins." Then he says to them, "Weep, but it will do you no good." And how many an old man puts his hand on his whiskers and laments for his old age and the length of his tribulation and the passing of his strength! How many a middle-aged one cries over the extent of his misfortune and the ignominy of his situation! How many a young person weeps for his youth and his sorrows and the loss of his beauty! How many a woman grabs onto her hair, crying out over her iniquity and /99/ rending her gown. And they all weep for a thousand years.

Then comes the call from God's direction, "O Mālik, drive them into the Fire through the first of its gates!" But just as the Fire is about to seize them, they all cry out together, "There is no God but God!" and the Fire flees from them a distance of five hundred years. They begin to sob, their voices rising in pitch, and then comes the call from God's direction, "O Fire, seize them! O Mālik, drive them into the Fire through the first of its gates!" At that they hear a great crashing noise, like the rumbling of thunder. Just as the Fire thinks that it is going to burn up their hearts, Mālik pushes it back, saying to it, "You will not consume a single heart in which the Qur'ān is to be found or which is a vessel of faith." When the guardians of hell come with boiling water to pour in their bellies, Mālik drives them away, saying, "Do not pour boiling water into a single belly which has hungered during Ramaḍān. The Fire will not burn the foreheads of any lowered in prostration before the Merciful." So they are turned back, charred like blackened sinners, but with their faith glimmering in their hearts. /100/

There is also the instance of a man in the Fire whose cries are so loud that his voice is raised above that of any other of its inhabitants. He comes out, burned black, and God says to him, "Why is your voice louder than that of any of the other people of the Fire?" He replies, "O Lord, You have held me accountable, but I have not given up hope of Your mercy!" So God says, "﴾Who despairs of the mercy of his Lord save those who have gone astray?﴿ [S 15:56] Go, for I have forgiven you."

And in the same manner a man goes out of the Fire and God says to him, "You have gone out of the Fire, but what have you done to enter the Garden? He answers, "O Lord, I ask You only for one small thing." So a tree is raised up for him from among the trees of the Garden, and God says to him, "Do you not see that if I gave you this tree you would ask Me for something else?" But he answers, "No, may You be glorified, O Lord!" So God says, "Then this is a gift from Me to you." But while he eats of it and finds shade under it, another tree is raised up by it even more lovely. The man cannot keep from looking at it, so God says, "What are you doing? Perhaps you would like it." And he says, "Yes, Lord." So God replies, "If I give it to you, you will just ask for something else." "No, may You be glorified, O Lord," the man insists. So God says, "It is a gift from Me to you." While he is eating /101/ of it and enjoying its shade, yet another tree is raised up for him, more lovely than either of the others. He cannot help looking at it, but his Lord forgives him, because it is impossible for him to have patience concerning that which he sees. Then God says, "Perhaps you would like it." And he answers, "Yes, O Lord." "But if I give it to you," says God, "you will surely ask me for something else." And the man insists again, "No, may You be glorified, O Lord. I will not ask for anything more." Then God smiles and leads him into the Garden, distributing to him of its property double what he had on earth. (I have mentioned similar stories in the Iḥyā'.)

In [a work entitled] Tartīb al-nasaq[139] it says that when God appears to the people He seizes the seven heavens in His right hand and the earths in His left. Thus is His word,﴾...He will seize the entire earth on the day of resurrection, and the heavens will be rolled up in His right hand...﴿ [S 39:67] At the moment of the rolling up, the noise of their splitting is greater than the crashing of rumbling thunder. Thus has He said, /102/ ⁋On that day We shall roll up the heaven like the rolling of the scroll [*al-sijill*] of the Book...⁋ [S 21:104] (*Al-sijill* is the name used for paper on which something is written; paper that has nothing written on it is called *qirṭās*.)

In a narrative of the Ṣaḥīḥ it says that God rolls up the earth just as one of you might roll up his bread for a journey. And another *ḥadīth* relates that the first nourishment that the people of the Garden will take is an abundance of the liver of the fish on which are found the seven earths.[140] It is grilled for them and given to them, along with the terrestrial earth, for on that day the earth will be like fresh bread. And in the Ṣaḥīḥ it is related that they enter the Garden with the stature of Adam,[141] smooth and beardless, their eyes anointed with kohl. On that day truth will be the measure. There is only the glance of an eye in time between the appearance of the two angels and the --------[142] form until the appearance of the Holy Form.[143]

And in /103/ some strange narratives about the ordinances of the hereafter it is related how people are brought to God, judged and reprimanded. Their good and evil deeds are weighed, during all of which it seems to each one that God certainly is not judging anyone else just then. In fact, however, it may be that at that instant thousands and thousands are being held to account, so many that they cannot be numbered except by God. And every one of them thinks that the reckoning is for him alone. In that way no one of them can see any of the others, nor hear what any other is saying; each one is under his own coverings. Glory be to Him to Whom belongs all of this, and glory be to Him Whose power and by the wonders of Whose wisdom it comes to pass. Frustrated, misguided and lost is he who magnifies other than God. This is the meaning of His saying, ⁋Your creation and your resurrection are only as an individual soul...❳ [S 31:28] He also said, ❲We shall dispose of you, O you two classes [of humans and *jinn*]❳ [S 55:31], one of the wondrous mysteries of al-Malakūt, for His dominion is limitless. Glory be to the One who does not allow any one concern to keep Him from attending to any other.

In this situation a man is brought to his son and he says to him, "O /104/ my son, I provided clothing for you when you had not the means to clothe yourself. And I gave you food and drink when you were incapable of getting it on your own. I sustained you as a young child when you were unable to ward off any adversity and obtain that which would benefit you. How many fruits would I have liked for myself, but I bought them for you instead! What you see is sufficient to show you the terror of the day of resurrection. Now the evil deeds of your father are many. Take from me some of them -- even one less would lighten my burden -- and give me even one good deed so that I might add it to my balance." But the son flees from him, saying, "I need them more than you do!" Thus it goes with families, friends and the like. For God has said, ❲On that day a man will flee from his brother and from his mother and from his father and from his wife and from his children.❳ [S 80:34-36]

In the Ṣaḥīḥ is a narrative telling that people will be resurrected naked. ᶜĀ'isha is reported to have said, "How shameful that they will see each other's nudity!" But the Prophet replied, /105/ "❲Each person on that day will have his own concern, causing him to be indifferent [to others].❳ [S 80:37]" The meaning here is that the intensity of their terror and the depth of their distress prevents them from looking at one another. When the people are all established on an equal footing, there rises up before them a black cloud, raining down pages all around them. The page intended for the believer is made of a rose petal, and that intended for a *kāfir* is a leaf of the lote-tree. All have writing on them, and they flutter out in every direction, some to the right and others to the left. It is not random, however, for [a page] falls to a person's right or his left, according to His word, *...We send out for him on the day of resurrection a Book, which he finds spread out.* [S 17:13] Even if one received it rolled up he would not find a place to spread it out because the creatures are all milling around, some of them attached to others.

One of the pious forefathers, a lettered man, related that people reach the Basin /106/ after passing the Ṣirāt, but he is mistaken in what he said, because one who has already crossed the Ṣirāt does not arrive at the Basin. It is on the seven bridges that most people perish.

As for the seventy thousand who enter the Garden without reckoning, no balance is raised up for them, nor are they given records [of their deeds]. Rather, they get a certificate of innocence on which are written the words: "There is no God but God; Muḥammad is the Messenger of God. This is the permit of Fulān ibn Fulān with which he can enter the Garden and is saved from the Fire." When God forgives him his sins, the angel takes him by his arm and shows him around the place of judgment, crying, "This is Fulān ibn Fulān. God has forgiven him his sins and given him such bliss that he will never again be miserable." Nothing more joyous than this standing has ever come to pass for him.

This same is done with him who is among the wretched, and for him nothing more calamitous has ever happened than having the angel say, "This is Fulān ibn Fulān. He is reduced to such misery that never again will he know any happiness." /107/ Nothing worse than this standing has ever come to pass for him.

On the day of resurrection the messengers will be on their thrones, and the Prophets and the *ᶜulamā'* will be on smaller thrones somewhat below them. The throne of each messenger will be in proportion to his rank or standing. The *ᶜulamā'* who have performed well will be on seats of light; the martyrs and the virtuous, such as the Qur'ān readers and those who give the call to prayer, will be on a mound made of musk. These pious groups are the possessors of chairs or seats; they are the ones who ask intercession from Adam and Noah until they come at last to the Messenger of God. All of these we have mentioned will come in person, hastening on the day of resurrection.

It is even said that the Qur'ān itself comes on the day of resurrection in the form of a man with a beautiful face and figure. He seeks permission to intercede, and it is granted. In the same way Islam comes to argue its cause, and is victorious. (We have mentioned the story of Islam along with ᶜUmar ibn al-Khaṭṭāb in the Kitāb al-Iḥyā'.) After it has pleaded its case, God joins whomever He wills to it, and Islam leads them to the Garden.

In that same way the world appears in the form /108/ of a hoary-haired old woman, as ugly as can be. The people are asked, "Do you recognize her?" and they answer, "We take refuge in God from her!" Then they are told, "This is the world, over which you used to envy and hate each other." In like manner Friday comes in the image of a bride being led in procession, as lovely as can be. The believers will gather around her, and all about them are mounds of musk and camphor, and on them will shine a light dazzling all who are at the place of resurrection until she leads them into the Garden.

Consider then -- may God have mercy on you -- the existence of the Qur'ān and Islam and Friday as personalities. On earth they are not understood to have individuality, but that belongs to the Malakūtī world.

The one who knows of this reality does not profess the creation of the Qur'ān, as did the Jahmīya,[144] who were ignorant of its Jabarūtī /109/ existence as a personality. Islam has a Malakūtī form, as do prayer, fasting and patience. He who knows that pays no heed to the one who argues that the soul is annihilated at death, just because the Prophet prayed at the Day of Trench,[145] "Oh our God, Lord of bodies consumed and transitory spirits!" and said to one who was visiting the tombs, "The dead man knows when the living visits him." These statements are taken out of context, and for each there is a wide latitude and flexibility of interpretation. We have mentioned them in other works; here only an abridged version is intended in order to follow the path of the *sunna*[146] and avoid the innovations that occur in the *sharīᶜa* inspired by the satans of mankind.[147]

We beseech God /110/ for immunity from error, help and guidance, by His grace and His favor. ⁅...Sufficient unto us is He, and most excellent is He in Whom we trust!⁆ [S 3:173] May God bless our master Muḥammad, his family and his companions, and give them peace in abundance.

The Precious Pearl is finished, written to unveil the knowledge of the hereafter, with praise to God, and by His grace and generosity.

Praise be to God, Lord of all the worlds!

NOTES

[1]As will be illustrated below, one of the rewards of virtue is the illumination of one's tomb during the period between death and resurrection.

[2]*Kufr* (and its agent *kāfir*) and *islām* (and its agent *muslim*) are very difficult to render by a one-word translation and will thus be kept in transliteration. *Kufr* is the act by which one rejects in ingratitude the signs and benefits of God and His messengers; *islām* is that act whereby one surrenders himself to God's will, and it at once signifies the community of those who have abandoned their own wills before God.

[3]S 3:185, 21:35 and 29:57.

[4]The term *malakūt* is used four times in the Qur'ān to mean power or dominion, e.g. "*malakūt al-samāwāt wa'l-arḍ*" [S 6:75], but with no reference to the *ᶜālam al-malakūt* or *jabarūt*. (*Jabarūt* also means might or greatness.) See Introduction, p. 7 , for a discussion of al-Ghazālī's use of these terms.

[5]This seems to refer to the usual distinction drawn between humans, animals and birds; see Qur'ān 6:38.

[6]*Jinn* is the generic name for the class of beings, or spirits, acknowledged by the Qur'ān to be created of fire and to come, like man, before God at the time of judgment.

[7]Al-Ghazālī consistently uses *kursī* rather than *ᶜarsh* to refer to the Throne of God, whose size encompasses the heavens and the earth. In the Qur'ān both words are used, and despite the attempts of the early exegetes to distinguish them, as well as later theological refinements, they generally can be said to

be synonymous. (*Kursī* is the term used in Qur'ān 2:256, the famous "Throne Verse" or *ayat al-kursī*.) A later distinction suggested that *kursī* refers to the seat itself, while *ᶜarsh* includes the pavilion on which it is set.

[8]Al-Ghazālī in this work most commonly refers to God as al-Jalāl and al-Jalīl, both of which mean He Who is majestic, glorious and sublime.

[9]Cf. al-Bayḍāwī, Tafsīr I, 351 (ed. Fleischer): "God stroked Adam's back and extracted from his loins his whole posterity, which should come into the world until the Resurrection, one generation after another..."

[10]This day of testimony and witness to the Lordship of God by His creatures (who are, in fact, not yet existent) is understood to be a kind of primordial covenant between man and God. It has been a favorite theme of meditation and inspiration for religious poetry in the mystical tradition of Islam. Modern Qur'ān commentary makes frequent reference to this verse, interpreting it to mean that because people are created by nature to know the truth there is no escape from individual accountability at the eschaton.

[11]The Qur'ān states clearly that each individual life on earth is of a specific and appointed duration [*ajal*], as in 6:2.

[12]While the Qur'ānic usages of the terms *nafs* and *rūḥ* shows them to be quite distinctly different, they soon came to be interchanged in common parlance, both referring to that part of the human constitution distinguishable from, though temporarily in union with, the body. Al-Ghazālī with few exceptions refers to the soul [*nafs*] of the one who has died rather than to his spirit [*rūḥ*]. In this instance, however, he does use spirit;

this apparent interchangeability is consistent with the Iḥyā' in which *nafs* and *rūḥ* are generally identified; see also pages 18, 20, 33, 34, 39 (also note 67) and 42 for uses of *rūḥ* in this context.

[13] The abbreviation *ṣlʿm* [*ṣallá Allāhu ʿalayhi wa-sallama*] is traditionally added at the mention of the Prophet Muḥammad. In the same way the author adds, as is the practice among Muslim writers, a phrase such as "may He be glorified and exalted" at nearly every mention of God, "may God's peace be upon him" at the mention of a prophet or messenger and "may God be pleased with him" after the name of the first four caliphs.

[14] Kaʿb al-Aḥbār was a Yemenī Jew who converted to Islam under Abū Bakr or ʿUmar; he is generally regarded as the prime authority for Jewish-Muslim tradition. His teachings were oral, and he is commonly cited by traditionists such as al-Ṭabarī.

[15] ʿĀ'isha was the daughter of Abū Bakr and was the Prophet's favorite wife (after Khadīja), whom he married when she was still a child. She came to play a very important role in the life of the Islamic community and is the reputed source of many traditions about the Prophet.

[16] These are the angels charged with casting the wicked into the Fire. They are described in Kitāb aḥwāl al-qiyāma (pp. 40-41) as follows: "There are nineteen letters in the *basmala*, and an equal number of *zabānīya*. They are called that because they work with their feet as well as their hands. They take ten thousand of the *kuffār* [rejectors] in each hand and each foot and are therefore able to punish forty thousand at one time.... Their eyes are like flashing lightening, their teeth are as white as cows' horns, their lips hang down to their feet and flames of fire issue from their mouths. Between

their shoulders is the distance of one year. And God has not created even one iota of mercy in their hearts." (See p. 17 of this text for al-Ghazālī's briefer descrip tion.)

[17]Iblīs is the Muslim equivalent of the Devil. In the Qur'ān he is the angel who refused to bow down befor Adam as God commanded him to do, for which insubordination he was banished from paradise and cursed by God. In some eschatological manuals it is said that the over-coming of Iblīs is one of the signs of the imminence of the Hour; as the exemplar of disobedience to the command of God he is doomed to destruction as a first step in the unfolding of the drama of judgment.

[18]Fulān in Arabic is the term for any unspecified person, as we might in English say "so-and-so." This translation will retain the term in transliteration.

[19]Jesus is called *al-masīḥ*, the Messiah, eleven times in the Qur'ān, although there is no elaboration of the term and it clearly does not retain the connotation understood by orthodox Christianity.

[20]Gabriel is one of the four archangels of Islam, whose primary function is to be the bearer of God's revelations to the prophets.

[21]Many traditions attributed to the Prophet make it clear that the dead person actually sees his soul depart, as the following cited by Mu. 11, 9 from Abū Hurayra: "Have you not noticed," said the Prophet, "how one stares fixedly when he dies?" "Oh yes," replied his listeners. "This is when he is watching his soul leave.

[22]*Al-Amīn*, the trustworthy or faithful one, is a title generally given to the angel Gabriel. Note below on page 17 of the text, however, that it is also used fo

Daqyā'īl, the angel who carries the soul of the profligate. This account of the ascent of Gabriel and the soul to the seven heavens, at the gate of each of which identification is sought and given, quite obviously parallels the ascent of Gabriel and the Prophet Muḥammad in the traditions concerning the *miʿrāj* (see note 57).

[23] There is not always unanimity among Muslim writers as to the location of particular angels in the various levels of heaven. Al-Qazwīnī's very interesting *ʿAjā'ib al-makhlūqāt* gives a lengthy tradition from Ibn ʿAbbās in which the angels of the seven heavens are in the form of cattle, hawks, eagles, green birds, *ḥūr al-ʿayn, al-waladān* (see note 69 below), and the sons of Adam, or humans, respectively. The angels assigned to these groups, again respectively, are Ismāʿīl, Mīkhā'īl. Ṣāʿadiyā'īl, Ṣalṣā'īl, Kalkā'īl, Samḥā'īl, and Rūbā'īl. Of these only Ṣalṣā'īl is mentioned by al-Ghazālī, and he is placed not in the fourth but in the lowest heaven.

[24] At the first five of these heavens described, the soul is commended respectively for his attendance to the five responsibilities that make up the "pillars" [*arkān*] of Islam, those duties enumerated by the Prophet as required of every Muslim: testimony of faith in God and His Messenger, prayer, almsgiving, fasting and pilgrimage. At the next two heavens he hears of his performance of additional meritorious acts.

[25] The Sidrat al-Muntahá is the name given to the lote-tree in the seventh heaven, whose shade covers the waters and the abode of the blessed. Some commentators assert that its root is in the sixth heaven and its limbs in the seventh, so great is its extent. Some Sufis claim to have attained to this height in the course of mystical experience, such as Abū Yazīd who is reported to have said, "I mounted the mount of sincerity which

lifted me up until I reached [the station of] love. Then I mounted the mount of longing by which I attained the heavens, then I mounted the mount of affection by which I attained to Sidrat al-Muntahá (*Maḥāsin al-majāli* p. 77 as quoted in Qassim al-Samarrai, *The Theme of Ascension* [1968], p. 234).

[26]Abū Muḥammad Yaḥyá ibn Aktham (d. 242 *hijrī*) was an orthodox Sunnī and preserver of traditions known for his learning, authority, knowledge of jurisprudence and literary skill. He was influential over the caliph al-Ma'mūn, and was appointed by him *qāḍī al-quḍāt* and administrator of public affairs. (Many traditions concerning this interesting figure are preserved in Ibn Kallikān's *Biographical Dictionary*, Vol. IV.)

[27]Islamic lore abounds with stories about people who have died and are seen in dreams by the living. Based on S 39:42 which describes God as taking unto Himself the souls of the sleepers and the dead, the sleep state has often been understood to be a time when the living and the dead actually share a common circumstance, a time when the departed may communicate with the living through the medium of dreams. (See Ibn Qayyim, *Kitab al-rūḥ*, pp. 28 sqq.; al-Suyūṭī, *Bushrá*, pp. 44-55.) Al-Ghazālī cites a number of these tales here; one may assume that in this text anyone seen in a dream is already dead. He himself is reported to have been seen in dreams numerous times after his death (Qazwīnī, *Āthār*, pp. 277-78). Belief in this phenomenon is still widely held, according to the Egyptian sociologist Sayyid ^{c}Uways (*Ḥadith ^{c}an al-thaqāfa* [1970], *al-Khulūd fī ḥayat al-Misriyyīn al-mu^{c}āsirīn* [1972].

[28]Abū Shihāb al-Zuhrī was a famous traditionist of the early Muslim community and a member of the court of the caliph ^{c}Abd al-Mālik (d. 742).

[29]^{c}Urwa ibn al-Zubayr, one of the earliest traditionists and an eminent authority in Medina, was a contemporary of al-Zuhrī; he was the brother of ^{c}Abd Allāh ibn Zubayr, pretender to the caliphate.

[30]Abū Yaḥyá ^{c}Abd al-Raḥīm ibn Muḥammad ibn Nubāta (d. 946) was court preacher under Sayf al-Dawla and renowned in Islam for the style and excellence of his sermons.

[31]Manṣūr ibn ^{c}Ammār ibn Kathīr, a native of either Basrá or Khurasan, was a collector and reciter of traditions in Iraq and Egypt. He was well-known for his eloquence in preaching as well as his wisdom and piety; he died in 225 *hijrī*.

[32]See below, pages 33 sqq., for an explanation of the stations.

[33]Another of the four archangels, ^{c}Izrā'īl is known as the angel of death. In this capacity he has final authority in the separation of the soul/spirit from the body, although it is God alone Who knows and signals the moment of each person's death. ^{c}Izrā'īl moves around the earth with the speed of light, seizing the souls of those whose appointed time has come.

[34]The description of the difference between the souls of the sinners and the faithful is drawn with even more vivid clarity in some of the traditions. Cf. Mishkāt I, 341: "But when an infidel is about to leave the world...the angel of death comes and sits at its head and says, 'Wicked soul, come out to displeasure from God.' Then it becomes dissipated in his body, and he seizes it, and when he does so they do not leave it in his hand for an instant, but put it in that hair-cloth and from it there comes forth a stench like the most offensive stench found on the face of the earth."

[35]This is a black basalt mountain north of Medina where the Prophet and his army lost a major battle to the Meccan Quraysh.

[36]*Sijjīn* is mentioned in the Qur'ān only in 83:7-8, ❨But no! Truly the book of the transgressors is in *sijjīn*, and what will explain to you what *sijjīn* is?❩ and is considered to be one of the so-called "mysterious words" of that Book. It has been variously interpreted as the place in which Iblīs is chained, and a rock underneath the bottom of the earth. It is also used as a proper name for the region of the Fire itself.

[37]Muᶜādh ibn Jabal, a Meccan, was a young convert to Islam who participated in the army of the Prophet in the battle of Badr and other of the early encounters; because of his proficiency in the Qur'ān he was sent by Muḥammad as a teacher to Yemen and elsewhere.

[38]Al-Ghazālī in this work does not dwell on a circumstance often elaborated in Islamic lore, that of the acute distress of the soul during and after the body's washing. It is quite clear that the dead are fully aware of the whole washing and shrouding process, as al-Suyūṭī supports by a variety of traditions in his Bushrá (p. 31). The general understanding is that the soul is intensely disturbed at its inability to participate in the affairs of the living, agonizing over its realization of final separation from things of this world. This is a theme one finds repeated over and again in different religious traditions. The belief that the soul remains in some way near the grave is a kind of remnant of pre-Islamic ideas, incorporated into the expanding fabric of Muslim theology concerning life after death. This particular set of beliefs is known as *aḥwāl al-qubūr*, the states of the graves.

[39]Rabīʿ ibn Khaytham was an early adherent of Islam; he died in the year 70 *hijrī*.

[40]Al-Ṣiddīq [the righteous, honest] (or al-Ṣadīq) refers to Abū Bakr, and al-Fārūq [he who distinguishes from falsehood] to ʿUmar ibn al-Khaṭṭāb, first and second caliphs of Islam respectively. ʿUthmān, next to be mentioned, was the third caliph.

[41]Compare the following from Ḥaqā'iq (IS 3, 503): "When the funeral bier has been placed on the edge of the grave, he is summoned by three (cries): 'Oh son of man, you were on me (= the earth) laughing, and you have come to be inside me weeping; you were on me rejoicing and you have come to be inside me grieving; you were on me speaking and you have come to be inside me silent.'"

[42]The history of accumulated layers of eschatological tradition is a perplexing study, the details of which are beyond this work. It seems, however, that Rūmān is a somewhat later appellation for the angel who serves the function described here. There is a certain confusion between this angel and the two mentioned in the next paragraph as the disturbers of the grave, which is not entirely cleared up in al-Ghazālī's treatment of the sequence of events.

[43]ʿAbd Allāh ibn Masʿūd was one of the first of the Meccans to accept the teachings of the Prophet and is famous for openly reciting the Qur'ān in Mecca. He became an authority on Qur'ān and tradition (d. 652-3?).

[44]At this point in the text the angels are not named, but it is clear from the next several pages that they are Munkar and Nakīr, the interrogating angels of the grave who are mentioned frequently in later Islamic texts, although they are referred to only once in

canonical tradition and not at all in the Qur'ān. The order of appearance of these angels is somewhat difficul to follow here, as they are introduced at this point, then announced again on page 25 by the personification of the works of the believer. The set of beliefs in Islamic theology dealing with the punishment meted out by these angels is called *ʿadhāb al-qabr*, the chastisement of the tomb.

[45]*ʿUlamā'*, the plural of *ʿālim* [one who has knowledge], refers to that body of scholars in Islam who have jurisprudence over questions of law and theology. It will be rendered in transliteration in this translation.

[46]There are many traditions that tell about the sequence of events after death in essentially the same order as al-Ghazālī has described them. Often the opening of a window or gate in the top of the tomb is followed by the expressed wish of the dead soul to have the interim pass quickly, as in A.b.H. IV, 296: "And when he sees what is in the Garden he says, 'Lord hasten the hour of resurrection that I may return to my people and my possessions!', but he is told, 'Abide here!'"

[47]The personification of one's deeds in Islamic tradition may well be simply another instance of the tendency to personify the abstract for didactic purposes. On the other hand, it is similar enough to the Zoroastrian concept of the female form of one's good and bad deeds coming on the third day after death that one might well look for influence here.

[48]*Al-Sāʿa*, the Hour, is a term commonly used for the day of judgment, specifically the time when humanity will be called to account. *Al-qiyāma* refers to the literal rising up at the resurrection, *baʿth* signifies the calling forth for judgment, and *ḥashr* is the gathering together. *Al-maʿād* (the return) is the general

term used by theologians for the entire process.

[49]This tree grows at the bottom of the Fire and is extremely bitter and unpleasant, with fruits like the heads of devils. (See Qur'ān 37:62-66).

[50]See Introduction, p. 5.

[51]This is a common theme in the traditions; Tir. 8:23 records the Prophet as having said, "He for whom there is wailing [*nawḥ*] is punished in accordance with the wailing done for him" and that of the four things left over from the Jāhilīya (the period of "ignorance" before the revelation of the Qur'ān), one is wailing. The primary offence seems to come not in lamentation as such, but in carrying to excess the demonstration of grief. "Loud lamenting is forbidden," says the Kitāb aḥwāl al-qiyāma (p. 30), "but there is no harm in crying over the dead, although it is better to be patient."

[52]This term has a range of meaning from heretic in the general sense in Islamic law to a Muslim who secretly professes the dualist principles of the Manichaeans. The latter is intended here, the reference being particularly to the rejection of the doctrine of the resurrection.

[53]The word translated as individuality is *al-ᶜayn*, literally the eye or the source. Here and in similar usage in this text it refers to the essence of one's personality.

[54]As Islamic theology and tradition developed, different and sometimes conflicting ideas concerning the fate of the individual between death and resurrection caused the total picture to become somewhat confused. Some of the variations are evident in this text. In general al-Ghazālī supports the idea that the souls of

both righteous and wicked remain in the grave until the Hour. The tradition here cited, a very well-known one based on the Qur'ānic assurance that those slain in the way of God are not dead but are still living [2:154], is an allusion to only one category of believer. This became expanded, however, so that one finds evidence in later traditions of the Prophet's having said that all souls of believers will be birds in the Garden awaiting the day of resurrection. Other references suggest that the *mu'minūn* will be on the right hand of Adam, at the Sidrat al-Muntahá (see note 25), in the seventh heaven, at the gates of the courtyard of the Garden, by the well of Zamzam. (See Ibn Qayyim al-Jawzīya, Kitāb al-rūḥ, pp. 134-73.)

[55] See Note 40 above.

[56] Ḥusayn, the second son of the Prophet's daughter Fāṭima and his cousin ᶜAlī, was massacred with his band of followers at Karbalā in Iraq in 680, an event still commemorated with great sorrow especially by Shīᶜa Islam.

[57] This is a reference to the night journey [*isrā'*] and ascension [*miᶜrāj*] to heaven referred to in Qur'ān 17:1 and greatly elaborated by Muslim tradition (see note 22). In most of the traditions about the *miᶜrāj* the Prophet is said to have met with others of God's messengers in the respective heavens and with Abraham in the seventh. The encounter with Jesus is usually said to have been in the second heaven, although al-Ghazālī here places him in the fifth.

[58] Literally the well-populated house, referring to the Kaᶜba (Qur'ān 52:4), or in this instance the celestial archtype of the earthly Kaᶜba.

[59] Respectively these titles refer to Abraham, Moses,

Jesus, Adam and Muḥammad.

[60]The Persian mystic Abū Yazīd al-Bisṭāmī (d. 261/875); see Note 25 above.

[61]There is some real disagreement in the traditions as to whether or not the dead will actually be recognized by other dead in the period before the resurrection. In the Bushrá, for instance, al-Suyūṭī cites several *ḥadīth*s similar to this narrative of al-Ghazālī's in which spirits of believers recognize the newly dead and ask him about their friends and families, then adds some that indicate that even when members of families meet they will be as strangers (p. 29). In the same way some traditions insist that the dead in the graves know those of the living who stop to greet them, while others say that they only have this recognition on Friday! (Bushrá, pp. 58-59).

[62]The region to which the profligate is sent is known by various terms in Islam, some of them pointedly graphic. *Hāwiya*, used here, means literally an abyss or deep hole whose bottom is endless. The most common term is *al-nār*, translated as the Fire. *Jahannam*, hell or the hell-fire with which God will punish the wicked and disobedient in the next life, is actually a proper name whose origin has been variously understood to be Arabic, Persian or Hebrew. Another of the proper names of the place of punishment is *saqar*, the fire of the world to come. Some say that it is a foreign word, and others that it is from the Arabic, meaning the sun scorched or burned him. (See Lane, Book I, pts. 2,4,8.)

[63]The Kharijites were one of the earliest sects of Islam, so-called because they seceded from the party of ᶜAlī. They are noted for their position on questions of the caliphate, faith and works, and legitimate membership in the Muslim community.

[64]See Qur'ān 2:30-34.

[65]See Note 10 above.

[66]*Barzakh* is a term that actually carries several possible meanings. Literally it is a separation or obstruction. It occurs in the Qur'ān three times (23:100, 25:53 and 55:20) and has been interpreted in eschatology as the barrier separating the Fire and Garden and/or the interval between the earthly death and the resurrection. For an excellent treatment of the various occurrences and usages of *barzakh* see R. Eklund's Life Between Death and Resurrection according to Islām (Uppsala, 1941).

[67]While all living things participate in the initial events of this day, God has breathed His spirit only into human beings and angels.

[68]This term, *al-qumqām*, is given in Ma^{c}lūf's al-Munjid as meaning the sea, or the greater part of it; its use here suggests a kind of farthest limit.

[69]The *ḥūr* are the beautiful chaste maidens of the Garden, named for their startling black eyes, who wait as rewards for virtuous male Muslims. They are specifically referred to in a number of passages in the Qur'ān. Less clearly identified in the Qur'ān but adopted into later tradition are the young men, also to be companions for the virtuous (although never suggested as partners for women as the *ḥūr* are for men).

[70]It is interesting to note that some of the earliest Qur'ānic references to death and resurrection are in the context of a dead land coming to life after receiving water from heaven (43:11, 35:9, 7:57).

[71] Cf. Mishkat II, 1165: "The only thing in a man which does not decay is one bone, the tail-bone, from which the whole frame will be reconstituted on the day of resurrection."

[72] Isrāfīl is a third archangel (Jibrīl and Izrā'īl have already been introduced; Mīkāl is the fourth) of enormous proportions. The first to be resurrected, according to tradition, he blows the horn described below and also announces the record of each individual as it is inscribed on the Guarded Tablet.

[73] The rock of the Temple of Jerusalem, over which the Dome of the Rock was built.

[74] See Note 67 above.

[75] The Arabic reads *bi-sāhira*, which in most English versions is translated as awake or awakened. Al-Ghazālī here, however, indicates that it refers to the leveling of the earth, which accords with al-Bayḍāwī's understanding that *sāhira* means a flat plain. (Anwār al-tanzīl, p. 729)

[76] Abū Sufyān, a caravan merchant, was one of the most influential of the tribe of Quraysh and a leader in the opposition to the Prophet. Under circumstances concerning which fact and legend are impossibly intermixed, he converted to Islam and later became a governor under Abū Bakr.

[77] The stress on proper shrouding of the dead is another recurrent theme in the *ḥadīth*s, as in Mu. II, 49 in which the Prophet, after having given specifics of burial, reasserts, "If any of you enshroud your brother, let him do it in the best possible manner!"

[78]That is, perhaps the Prophet meant not that Moses will avoid the circumstance of having no body, but rather that he may be exempt from the terrible dread that will take hold of all souls at that time, which al-Ghazālī goes on to describe.

[79]See Note 40 above.

[80]Al-Ghazālī's amplification of the Qur'ānic reference to one's light here is an example of the frequent use of light imagery in his writings. Actually somewhat gnostic in this understanding, he generally identifies light with knowledge and darkness with ignorance. The real light, of course, is al-Ḥaqq or God, and here the degree of light accompanying each individual is in direct proportion to his knowledge of and faith in God. The light one possesses is the determinant of the speed with which he can pass over the bridge of Ṣirāṭ (see Note 123 below), those with intense light flying over in an instant and those with very weak light crawling and groping across.

[81]*Al-Mahshar*, literally the place of congregation, is used for the place and time of the great gathering-together of all creatures at the resurrection.

[82]It is interesting to compare this with the legendary experience of the young Siddhārtha Gautama (who later became the Buddha) in which his first sight of old age, disease, death and poverty led him to the great renunciation.

[83]*Gharīb al-rawāya*, which probably refers to a *ḥadīth* with an unusual chain of reporters, i. e. one classified as "strange" with regard to its *isnād*.

[84]In the verse, this phrase follows directly the one quoted just above.

[85]Al-Karīm, another of the names of God.

[86]The *ᶜūd* is a musical instrument similar to a lute.

[87]This is apparently a reference to the animal formed of one's deeds on which he rides at the day of resurrection. See above pages 49-50.

[88]This sweating is greatly elaborated in some of the traditions, as when A.b.H. (IV, 157) cites the Prophet as having said that when the sun gets close to the earth people will sweat, and they will be in sweat up to their ankles, calves, knees, rumps, waists, shoulders and mouths, and some will be entirely covered by sweat.

[89]The singular *minbar* is most commonly translated pulpit, and in the mosque is the rostrum from which the Friday sermon is delivered. To avoid confusion with this image, the word has been translated in this text as throne, and refers to the station or platform of some of God's chosen at the place of resurrection, as will be illustrated in the text.

[90]Abū ᶜAlī al-Fuḍayl ibn ᶜIyāḍ (d. 803), a disciple of Sufyān al-Thawrī, was one of the early Sufis as well as a traditionist. He was noted for his asceticism and other-worldly concerns.

[91]Among the many delights of the Garden described in various places in the Qur'ān, the flowing rivers are conspicuous for the frequency of their mention. See, for example, 47:15, ﴿[Here is] a parable of the Garden which has been promised to the righteous, in which are rivers of pure water and rivers of milk whose taste never changes and rivers of wine, a delight for those who drink thereof, and rivers of clear honey...﴾.

[92]The role of children in the Garden is seldom, if

ever, articulated as an item of doctrine. There are many traditions that support the idea that children will be present in some capacity. "On the day of resurrection the child of the woman who has just given birth will drag her by his navel cord into the Garden." (Tay. No. 578) "Every child born in Islam is in the Garden full and happy, and says, 'Oh God, bring to me my parents!'" (Bushrá, p. 75) The traditions, of course, are replete with descriptions of the sensual joys (only occasionally understood allegorically) of the hereafter; a commonly cited *ḥadīth* is that found in A.b.H. III, 80: "If the believer desires a son in the Garden, conception and birth will take place in one hour." This is often accompanied, however, by the assertion that one will not so desire, and even that "The people of the Garden will have no children." (Khān, Ḥusn al-uswa, p. 219)

[93]The *nāqūr* is mentioned in the Qur'an only in 74:8-9, ‡For then the horn will be sounded, and that day will be a difficult day‡. The trumpet is mentioned as *al-ṣūr* in 6:73, 23:101, 39:68 and 69:13.

[94]Qur'ān 2:35-36.

[95]In Islam a distinction is drawn between a prophet [*nabīy*] and a messenger [*rasūl*]. All messengers are prophets, meaning that they are bearers of God's message to men, but the *rasūl* has a wider significance. There are twenty-eight prophets mentioned in the Qur'ān, while the following are accorded the status of *rasūl*; Noah, Lot, Ishmael, Moses, Shuʿayb, Hūd, Ṣāliḥ, Jesus and Muḥammad.

[96]The Qur'ānic picture of Noah does not show him to be culpable in any way; in fact he himself is greatly put upon by the torments of his countrymen. The allusion here seems to be his having said, as in *sūra* 23:26, ‡My

Lord help me, for they accuse me of deceit!*, after which God taught him how to build the ark.

[97]Qur'ān 6:76-8 indicates that Abraham mistook a star, the moon and the sun in turn for his Lord.

[98]Years here refers to the time of the drought; see Qur'ān 7:130.

[99]Qur'ān 28:15-21 relates the story of Moses (accidently) killing an Egyptian who was fighting with an Israelite.

[100]This refers, of course, to the deification of Jesus and the near-deification of his mother Mary by the Christians, always anathema to Muslims.

[101]The seal [*khātim*] is the traditional designation of the Prophet Muḥammad as the last in the line of prophets. See Qur'ān 33:40.

[102]When the Prophet joined the battle against the Quraysh near Uḥud (see Note 35 above) he was struck in the face by a rock which knocked out his tooth.

[103]Muḥammad was frequently accused by his adversaries of being a soothsayer [*kāhin*] or of being *majnūn*, inspired by the *jinn* rather than having received revelations from God (e.g., Qur'ān 15:6).

[104]Al-Ṣiddīq in this instance refers not to Abū Bakr (see above Note 40) but to Joseph, as he was addressed by the cupbearer in *sūra* 12:46.

[105]The question of whether or not anyone can mediate or intercede with God on the day of judgment was one of the most hotly debated issues of early Islamic theology. For the most part the Qur'ān insists that no one can intercede on that day, but orthodoxy finally accepted the

mediation of the Prophet, as expressed in the Waṣiyat Abī Ḥanīfa, Article 25: "The intercession of our Prophet Muḥammad (may Allah give him blessing and peace) is a reality for all those who belong to the inhabitants of Paradise, even if they should be guilty of mortal sins." (Wensinck, The Muslim Creed, p. 130)

[106] *Zabībatān* signifies the two small black spots found above the eyes of serpents, or two collections of foam which form on the sides of its mouth when it is angry. (Lane, Book I, pt. 3)

[107] I.e., judge their merits and demerits (for they have been waiting for the judgment for a very long time).

[108] From this point on in the text, and in the progression of events, distances are measured in terms of time rather than space.

[109] The one [to be] slaughtered. The story of the would-be sacrifice of Abraham's son is a popular one in Islam, but most Muslims assert that it was Ishmael who volunteered himself to be the sacrifice. He is thus called the slaughtered, although a ram was substituted. See Qur'ān 19:54, ❴And mention in the Book Ismāʿīl, for he was true to his promise...❵

[110] This rather surprising occurrence is based on the Qur'ān verse that al-Ghazālī cites immediately below. It is specified in a variety of traditions, including the one he notes of al-Bukhārī (65:68, 97:24), that of Aḥmad ibn Ḥanbal (III, 16) and others. It is put into context in a long tradition cited by Ṭayālisī (pp. 289-90) in which God speaks first with the misled peoples of the Book and then with the true worshippers of God at the day of resurrection. They assure Him that they have lived righteously on earth and are now awaiting God. He asks if there will be a sign by which He can be recognized,

and when given an affirmative reply proceeds to provide that sign by uncovering His leg.

111 Al-Ghazālī is here supporting the orthodox conclusion that (despite the assertions of the Mu^{c}tāzila and many of the philosophers) the specifics of the day of resurrection are not to be understood allegorically.

112 In the philosophical sense [*a^{c}rāḍ*].

113 While the beasts and birds are present at the day of judgment, actual settlement is made only between those animals that have done harm to each other (as specifically stated here, with their horns), and then all fade away into dust.

114 The peoples of ^{c}Ād and Thamūd (mentioned in the next paragraph) are referred to frequently in the Qur'ān as examples of those who suffered God's punishing wrath, as a result of their rejection of the message of the prophets Hūd and Ṣāliḥ, sent to them respectively (see Note 95 above).

115 The text is faulty at this point and it seems impossible to ascertain the particular peoples to whom the author is referring. Gautier, who consulted several manuscripts in the preparation of his French translation (see Introduction, pp. 9-10), concludes that "Les noms de ces peuples sont intelligibles et les mss. présentent des leçons très variées dont on peut affirmer pourtant l'origine commune." (<u>La Perle Précieuse</u>, p. 62, n. 5)

116 Muslim writers have generally used the name Tubba^{c} for the kings of the Ḥimyarites, the dynasty that succeeded Saba in South Arabia after the destruction of the famous Dam of Ma^{c}rib. The Qur'ān speaks twice of the companions of al-Rass (25:38, 50:12), but it is not clear exactly to whom this refers; some have assumed it

means the people of Shuʿayb, while others suggest the town of al-Rass in the center of the Arabian Penninsula.

[117]*Tābūt al-sakīna*, also used as a construct to mean purity of the heart. This person here indicated is identified below as Uriah, whom David sent into battle so that he could marry his wife Bathsheba (a non-Qur'ānic legend found in the Old Testament in II Samuel).

[118]That is, in retribution for the wrong David did to Uriah.

[119]The traditions are replete with descriptions particularly of the *ḥūr*, black-eyed maidens awaiting in pearl-encrusted domiciles, who will be the reward of the virtuous in the Garden. Since up to one hundred a night are promised to the faithful, one can assume that it is not intended that David should be totally deprived of these pleasures.

[120]Abū Saʿīd ʿAbd al-Mālik ibn Qurayb al-Aṣmaʿī (d. 828) was a famous philologist of the Arabic language, skilled in the study of grammar, lexicography and poetry.

[121]Cf. Qur'ān 96:15.

[122]See Note 52 above.

[123]Al-Ṣirāṭ as meaning path or way is mentioned numerous times in the Qur'ān. Only two of these references, S 36:66 and 37:23 have normally been cited as supportive of the idea that there is a bridge to or over Hell (the latter reference is to the *ṣirāṭ al-jaḥīm*). Tradition came to include passage over this bridge for both the saved and the condemned as a necessary step in the events of the day of resurrection. For the faithful the way is broad and passage is easy; for the wrong-doers the bridge becomes razor-thin and finer than a hair, from which they fall into the Fires of

punishment. See A.b.Ḥ. II, 533 sq.

[124]Literally "the high places", this is the title of the seventh *sūra* of the Qur'ān and is used specifically in 7:46 sqq. where the companions of the heights [*aṣḥāb al-aᶜrāf*] are described. The meaning of *al-aᶜrāf* has long been disputed; the companions have been variously identified as angels, martyrs, the children of Muslims, etc. The most common explanation is that they are persons whose good and bad deeds are equal, and that the heights serves as a kind of limbo between the Garden and the Fire.

[125]This work to which the author refers is apparently not extant; there is no mention of it in Brockelmann nor in other listings of the works of al-Ghazālī available to us.

[126]The Basin, not mentioned in the Qur'ān, is another of the eschatological realities described in the traditions. Al-Ghazālī gives some suggestion of its dimensions here; it is reputed to be the place where the Prophet will intercede for his community on the day of resurrection, as the author suggests at the end of the paragraph.

[127]See *sūra* 108:1, ❴We have given to you *al-kawthar*.❵ Thus mentioned with no elaboration in the Qur'ān, this river is described in the *ḥadīth*s as a river of the Garden shown to the Prophet on his night journey and ascent. (It is also sometimes identified with the Basin of the Prophet.) Later traditions elaborate earlier descriptions by saying it has banks of gold and a bed of precious jewels. More symbolic interpretation understands Kawthar to be the source of God's beneficience and mercy.

[128]For example Solomon and Job, as in Qur'ān 38:30, 44.

[129]Some later commentators have said that Shuᶜayb, mentioned three times in the Qur'ān (7:85-93, 11:84-95 and 29:36-37), is to be identified with Moses' father-in-law Jethro, although this is not generally accepted; in the Qur'ān he is a prophet (and also a messenger), after Hūd and Ṣāliḥ, sent to Midian. He is reputed later to have gone blind.

[130]ᶜAbd Allāh ibn ᶜAbbās, the Prophet's cousin, son of the progenitor of the ᶜAbbāsid line and a much venerated traditionist. His ability in exposition was often lauded, as in the famous saying of Ibn Masᶜūd, "Indeed, Ibn ᶜAbbās is the interpreter [*tarjumān*] of the Qur'ān!"

[131]The *umma* or community of the Prophet.

[132]ᶜAqīl ibn Abī Ṭālib was the older brother of ᶜAlī (see Note 133 below). He is best known through the sources as an authority on geneologies and Quraysh history, and as a powerful and eloquent speaker.

[133]Cousin of the Prophet, fourth caliph of Islam and the first of the ᶜAlid *imāms* of the party of the Shīᶜa. He married the Prophet's daughter Fāṭima and received from Muḥammad the surname Abū Turāb.

[134]It is interesting to note here that the stress is less on the virtue of charity, according to which one might expect the Messiah to give his mug and comb to the needy, than on simple austerity.

[135] *Al-kabā'ir* [sing. *kabīra*] is the term accepted in Muslim theology for major transgressions, or grave sins (based on Qur'ān 42:37). There has seldom been

absolute consensus among the theologians, however, as to precisely which acts fall into this category, or what is the final fate of those who commit such transgressions. One act, though, is universally accepted in Islam as *kabīra*, that of *shirk* or association of anything with God.

[136]Al-Ḥasan al-Baṣrī, a first century ascetic and traditionist, is particularly well-known for his piety and is often considered a forerunner of the Sufis. He is renowned for his extreme terror of the punishments of the hereafter, which is reflected in this wish to be the one who suffers only for a thousand years rather than more.

[137]Meaning literally dirt or filth, *uff* is used as an expression of annoyance, deep disgust or even hatred.

[138]Mālik is the angel who oversees the region of the Fire; see Qur'ān 43:77.

[139]Literally "the order of arrangement".

[140]Quite a few traditions mention the eating of this fish liver (as A.b.H. III, 108: "The first thing that the people of the Garden will eat is the abundance of fish liver...") without identifying the fish as the creature on which the earth or earths are found. Gautier (p. 84) notes a tradition cited by Ibn Qutayba as saying that "the earth is on the back of a fish, and the people of the Garden eat of its liver upon first entering [the Garden]."

[141]Given here as *ᶜalá qāmati Adam*, this tradition is sometimes rendered by *ᶜalá ṣūrati*, as in that cited by Pocock in which the height of Adam's form is given as sixty cubits. (Twells, The Theological Works of the

<u>Learned Dr. Pocock</u>, Vol. I, p. 235)

[142]The Arabic reads *maʿmūra*, the built-up. It is possible that the text is misprinted and that the original was *maʿmūla*, assumed.

[143]See page 81 above.

[144]Named after Jahm ibn Ṣafwān (executed in 745), the Jahmīya shared many articles of faith with the Muʿtazila, including the denial of anthropomorphic attributes of God and affirmation of the createdness of the Qur'ān.

[145]Known as the siege of Medina, or the battle of the trench [*khandaq*], this skirmish began in March of 627. It was a significant victory of the followers of Muḥammad over their Meccan adversaries, achieved through the strategem of digging a trench as fortification around their army.

[146]Literally custom or way, *sunna* most commonly refers to those practices that the Prophet followed or advised his community to follow. Technically it includes his acts, words, and the things to which he gave approval.

[147]See Qur'ān 6:112, ﴾Thus We made for every prophet an enemy -- satans of men and *jinn*...﴿

REFERENCES

al-Bayjūrī, Ibrāhīm. Sharḥ al-Bayjūrī ᶜalā'l-jawhara. Cairo, 1964.

al-Bayḍāwī, ᶜAbd Allāh b. ᶜUmar. Anwār al-tanzīl wa-asrār al-ta'wīl. Cairo: Kutub al-Jumhūrīya al-ᶜArabīya, n.d.

Brockelmann, Carl. Geschichte der arabischen Litteratur. Zweite den Supplementbaenden angepasste Auflage. Leiden: E. J. Brill, 1937-1942, 3 voll. [GAL]

al-Bukhārī, Abū ᶜAbd Allāh Muḥammad b. Ismāᶜīl. Al-Jāmiᶜ al-ṣāḥīḥ. Cairo: Dār Iḥyā' Kutub al-Sunna, 1966, 4 voll. [Bu.]

Ad-Dourra al-Fākhira: La Perle Precieuse de Ghazālī. Traité d'Eschatologie Musulmane, avec une traduction française par Lucien Gautier. Leipzig: Otto Harrassowitz, 1925 (réimpression de l'édition Genève 1878).

Eklund, Ragnar. Life Between Death and Resurrection According to Islam. Uppsala: Almqvist and Wiksells Boktryckeri-A.-B., 1941.

Fā'iz, Aḥmad. al-Yawm al-ākhir fī ẓilāl al-Qur'ān. Beirut, 1975.

al-Ghazālī, Abū Ḥāmid Muḥammad b. Muḥammad. Iḥyā' ᶜulūm al-dīn. Cairo, 1334 *hijri*, 4 voll.

Ibn Ḥanbal, Aḥmad b. Muḥammad. Musnad. Cairo: al-Maṭbaᶜa al-Maymanīya, 1875, 6 voll. [A.b.Ḥ.]

Ibn Khallikān, Aḥmad b. Muḥammad. Wafayāt al-aᶜyān wa-anbā' abnā' al-zamān. Wm. Macguckin de Slane, Transl. Paris: Oriental Translation Fund of G.-B. and Ireland, 1843-1861, 4 voll.

Ibn Qayyim al-Jawzīya. Hādī al-arwāḥ. Cairo: Maydān al-Azhar, n.d.

--------. Kitāb al-rūḥ. Cairo: Dār al-Maᶜārif, 1357 *hijrī*.

Khalīfa, Muḥammad ᶜAbd al-Ẓāhir. Kitāb al-dār al-barzakhīya. Cairo: Maṭbaᶜat Ḥasan, 1973.

Khān, Ṣadīq Ḥasan. Ḥusn al-uswa. Cairo, n.d.

Kitāb aḥwāl al-qiyāma. An anonymous text translated by M. Wolff as Muhammedanische Eschatologie. Leipzig: F. A. Brockhaus, 1872.

Kitāb ḥaqā'iq al-daqā'iq of Abū'l-Layth al-Samarqandī. Translation in part with accompanying explanation by John Macdonald in Islamic Studies 3 (1964) and 4 (1965).

Lane, E. W. An Arabic-English Lexicon. London: Williams and Norgate, 1863-93, 1 vol. in 8.

Lazarus-Yafeh, Hava. Studies in Al-Ghazzali. Jerusalem: Magnes Press, The Hebrew University, 1975.

Līmūd, Ḥāmid Maḥmūd. Jawhar al-tawḥīd. Cairo, 1974.

Mishkāt al-maṣābīḥ. Edition and translation by James Robson of al-Baghawī's collection of the traditions of Muḥammad. Lahore: Sh. Muhammad Ashraf, 1965, 2 voll.

Muslim b. al-Ḥajjāj, Abū'l-Ḥusayn. Ṣāḥīḥ Muslim. Cairo: Dār Iḥyā' al-Kutub al-ᶜArabīya, 1955-56, 5 voll. [Mu.]

Qazwīnī, Zakariyā' Muḥammad b. Muḥammad. Āthār al-bilād. Ed. F. Wüstenfeld. Göttingen, 1847.

--------. Kitāb ᶜajā'ib al-mukhlūqāt wa-gharā'ib al-mawjūdāt. Ed. F. Wüstenfeld. Göttingen, 1849.

Quṭb, Sayyid. Mashāhid al-qiyāma fī'l-Qur'ān. Cairo: Dār al-Maᶜārif, 1961.

al-Samarrai, Qassim. *The theme of Ascension in Mystical Writings*. Baghdad: National Printing and Publishing Co., 1968

Smith, Margaret, *Al-Ghazālī the Mystic*. London: Luzac and Co., 1944.

al-Suyūṭī, al-Imām Jalāl al-Dīn. *Bushrá al-ka'īb bi-liqā' al-ḥabīb*. Cairo, 1969.

al-Ṭayālisī, Muḥammad b. Jaʿfar. *Musnad*. Haydarabad: Maṭbaʿat Majlis Dā'irat al-Maʿārif al-Niẓāmīya, 1904.

al-Tirmidhī, Abū ʿĪsá Muḥammad b. ʿĪsá. *al-Jāmiʿ al-ṣaḥīḥ*. Cairo: Maṭbaʿat al-Ḥalabī, 1937, 2 voll.

ʿUways, Sayyid. *Ḥadīth ʿan al-thaqāfa*. Cairo, 1970.

--------. *Al-Khulūd fī ḥayāt al-miṣrīyīn al-muʿāṣirīn*. Cairo: al-Hay'a al-Miṣrīya al-ʿĀmma li'l-Kitāb, 1972.

Wensinck, A. J. *Concordance et indices de la tradition musulmane*. Leiden: Brill, 1936-69, 7 voll.

--------. *The Muslim Creed*. New York: Barnes and Noble, Inc., 1965.

INDEX

(Numbers refer to pages of the manuscript text rather than of the translation.)